PERFORMANCE STANDARDS FOR ELECTRONIC CHART DISPLAY
AND INFORMATION SYSTEMS (ECDIS)
AND ECDIS—GUIDANCE FOR GOOD PRACTICE

国际海事组织
ECDIS性能标准与良好实践指南
2024版

交通运输部南海航海保障中心◎编译

·广州·

版权所有 翻印必究

图书在版编目（CIP）数据

国际海事组织 ECDIS 性能标准与良好实践指南：2024版：汉文、英文 / 交通运输部南海航海保障中心编译. --广州：中山大学出版社，2025.7. -- ISBN 978-7-306-08490-3

Ⅰ. U692.2；U675.81

中国国家版本馆 CIP 数据核字第 2025L4A252 号

出 版 人：	王天琪
策划编辑：	张 蕊
责任编辑：	杨曼琪
封面设计：	曾 婷
责任校对：	陈书坤
责任技编：	靳晓虹
出版发行：	中山大学出版社
电　　话：	编辑部 020 - 84110283，84113349，84111997，84110779，84110776
	发行部 020 - 84111998，84111981，84111160
地　　址：	广州市新港西路 135 号
邮　　编：	510275　　传　　真：020 - 84036565
网　　址：	http://www.zsup.com.cn　E-mail：zdcbs@mail.sysu.edu.cn
印 刷 者：	广州小明数码印刷有限公司
规　　格：	787mm×1092mm　1/16　8.625 印张　167 千字
版次印次：	2025 年 7 月第 1 版　2025 年 7 月第 1 次印刷
定　　价：	36.00 元

如发现本书因印装质量影响阅读，请与出版社发行部联系调换

《国际海事组织 ECDIS 性能标准与良好实践指南（2024版）》编译委员会

主 任 委 员：李宏印

副主任委员：洪四雄

委　　　员：李文华　王　平　孙　冰　李　伟
　　　　　　　杨　毅　刘　锋

翻　　　译：巫炳臻　李妍娜　潜成胜　吴晓婷

审　　　校：杨　毅　刘　锋　邬　金　余锦超
　　　　　　　罗子汶　马永学

编者的话

《国际海事组织 ECDIS 性能标准与良好实践指南（2024 版）》收录了国际海事组织（International Maritime Organization, IMO）有关船载电子海图显示与信息系统（electronic chart display and information system, ECDIS）的两份标准/指南，即《ECDIS 性能标准》与《ECDIS 良好实践指南》。

ECDIS 是依据《国际海上人命安全公约》（International Convention for the Safety of Life at Sea，以下简称《SOLAS 公约》）要求，国际航行船舶必须配备的船载电子海图导航和辅助决策系统。ECDIS 通过使用船载雷达（radar）、计程仪（doppler log）、全球定位系统（global positioning system, GPS）、电罗经（gyro）、船舶自动识别系统（automatic identification system, AIS）、航行警告系统（navigational telex, NAVTEX）、测深仪（echo sounder）、航行数据记录仪（voyage data recorder, VDR）、自动舵（autopilot）等设备，对各类信息进行采集和综合处理，并将其显示在电子海图设备上。ECDIS 可以有选择地显示电子航行海图中的信息以及从航行传感器获得的各类信息，通过各处理单元进行综合处理和显示，帮助航海人员进行航线设计和航路监视，并能按要求显示其他与航海相关的补充信息的信息系统，在保障船舶航行安全和提高航行效率方面发挥着关键作用。

《ECDIS 性能标准》是 IMO 规定的符合《SOLAS 公约》要求的 ECDIS 必须满足的性能标准，《ECDIS 良好实践指南》则能为航海人员良好地使用 ECDIS 提供指引。两份标准/指南均在 2024 年 IMO 海上安全委员会上通过了最新修订版本，本次修订增加了对最新的"通用海道测量数据模型（S-100）"标准数据的要求等内容。IMO 成员国和《SOLAS 公约》缔约国政府关注并有效落实相关的要求，计划将于 2026 年 1 月 1 日起开始执行，于 2029 年 1 月 1 日实现全面执行。

我国是 IMO A 类理事国，也是《SOLAS 公约》缔约国，本书的编译，有利于我国政府切实履行公约要求，便于我国航海界更好地理解《ECDIS 性能标准》的最新要求，也有利于广大船舶用户落实《ECDIS 良好实践指南》的最新要求。

本书目标读者包括交通运输、海事系统工作人员，国际海事组织跟踪人员，海事管理信息化人员，航运企业从业人员，航海安全保障人员，船舶检验人员，船载设备厂商，航海信息系统开发工程师，港口、引航、搜救相关从业者等。

目 录

ECDIS 性能标准

电子海图显示和信息系统（ECDIS）性能标准 ·············· 2
  附件　电子海图显示和信息系统（ECDIS）性能标准 ·············· 4
    附录 1　参考文件 ·············· 15
    附录 2　可用于航线规划和航线监控显示的系统数据库信息 ············ 18
    附录 3　导航要素和参数 ·············· 20
    附录 4　有特殊条件的区域 ·············· 21
    附录 5　警报和提示标识 ·············· 22
    附录 6　备用系统配置要求 ·············· 24
    附录 7　栅格海图显示系统（RCDS）操作模式 ·············· 27

PERFORMANCE STANDARDS FOR ELECTRONIC CHART DISPLAY AND INFORMATION SYSTEMS (ECDIS) ········ 32

ANNEX　PERFORMANCE STANDARDS FOR ELECTRONIC CHART DISPLAY AND INFORMATION SYSTEMS (ECDIS) ············ 35
  APPENDIX 1　REFERENCE DOCUMENTS ·············· 49
  APPENDIX 2　SYSTEM DATABASE INFORMATION AVAILABLE FOR DISPLAY DURING ROUTE PLANNING AND ROUTE MONITORING ·············· 52
  APPENDIX 3　NAVIGATIONAL ELEMENTS AND PARAMETERS ······ 54
  APPENDIX 4　AREAS FOR WHICH SPECIAL CONDITIONS EXIST ····· 55
  APPENDIX 5　ALERTS AND INDICATORS ·············· 56
  APPENDIX 6　BACKUP REQUIREMENTS ·············· 58
  APPENDIX 7　RCDS MODE OF OPERATION ·············· 62

ECDIS 良好实践指南

海上安全委员会通函草案　ECDIS 良好实践指南	70
附件　ECDIS 良好实践指南（第 2 次修订版）	72
附录 1　ECDIS 显示操作和显示异常清单（不按优先级排序）	80
附录 2　栅格海图显示系统（RCDS）和 ECDIS 的区别	84
附录 3　ECDIS 模拟器的操作培训和评估指南	85
附录 4　ECDIS 更新操作示例	94
参考文件	96

DRAFT MSC CIRCULAR ECDIS—GUIDANCE FOR GOOD PRACTICE ……… 97
ANNEX ECDIS—GUIDANCE FOR GOOD PRACTICE（REVISION 2） ……… 99

APPENDIX 1　LIST OF ECDIS APPARENT OPERATING AND DISPLAY ANOMALIES（NOT IN PRIORITY ORDER）	109
APPENDIX 2　DIFFERENCES BETWEEN RASTER CHART DISPLAY SYSTEM（RCDS）AND ECDIS	113
APPENDIX 3　GUIDANCE ON TRAINING AND ASSESSMENT IN THE OPERATIONAL USE OF ECDIS SIMULATORS	115
APPENDIX 4　EXAMPLES OF ONBOARD ECDIS UPDATES	126
REFERENCES	128

ECDIS 性能标准

电子海图显示和信息系统（ECDIS）性能标准

MSC.530（106）/REV.1 号决议
（2024 年 5 月 24 日通过）

　　海上安全委员会（MSC），根据《国际海事组织公约》第 28 条（b）款关于本委员会职能的规定；根据 A.886（21）号决议，即大会决定应视具体情况由海上安全委员会和/或海上环境保护委员会代表国际海事组织履行通过性能标准和技术规格及其修订的职能；根据 1974 年《国际海上人命安全公约》（以下简称《SOLAS 公约》）第 V/19 条和 V/27 条，即要求所有船舶须配备足够且最新的海图、航行指南、灯标表、航海通告、潮汐表以及计划航程所必需的所有其他航海出版物；根据经修正的 A.817（19）号决议和 MSC.232（82）号决议，即规定了电子海图显示和信息系统（ECDIS）性能标准的决议；注意到《SOLAS 公约》第 V/19 条和 V/27 条要求的最新海图可在船上通过 ECDIS 以电子化方式提供并显示，且第 V/27 条要求的其他航海出版物也可用这种方式提供和显示；注意到 ECDIS 技术的最新发展和功能强化，包括性能标准中新增的电子海图传输功能，是实施协调海事服务的电子导航概念的必要步骤；认识到有必要提高之前由 MSC.232（82）号决议通过的经修订的 ECDIS 性能标准，以确保此种设备的运行可靠性，并考虑到科技进步和实践经验，通过了 MSC.530（106）号决议，并引入国际海道测量组织（IHO）S-100 系列标准的新一代技术规范；认识到通过规范船舶航线规划的标准化数字交换，有利于进一步提高性能标准的益处；根据本组织已通过的在船载自动识别系统（AIS）范围内，船—岸与岸—船静态和动态航程信息交换的操作指南，审议了航行、通信和搜救分委会在其第 10 次会议上提出的建议。

　　1. 通过经修订的《电子海图显示和信息系统（ECDIS）性能标准》，其文本载于本决议的附件。

　　2. 建议各缔约国政府确保 ECDIS 设备满足以下要求：

　　（a）在 2029 年 1 月 1 日及之后安装的设备，其性能标准不得低于本决议附件规定；

　　（b）在 2026 年 1 月 1 日至 2029 年 1 月 1 日前安装的设备，其性能标准不得低于本决议附件或 MSC.232（82）号决议附件规定；

　　（c）在 2009 年 1 月 1 日至 2026 年 1 月 1 日前安装的设备，其性能标准不

得低于 MSC.232（82）号决议附件规定；和

（d）在 1996 年 1 月 1 日至 2009 年 1 月 1 日前安装的设备，其性能标准不得低于经 MSC.64（67）号和 MSC.86（70）号决议修订的 A.817（19）号决议附件规定。

3. 同意本决议中，"在 2029 年 1 月 1 日及之后安装"系指：

（a）在 2029 年 1 月 1 日及之后签订建造合同的船舶；或在无建造合同的情况下，在 2029 年 1 月 1 日及之后建造的船舶，设备在船上的任何安装日期；或

（b）上述（a）项以外的船舶，设备的合同交付日期在 2029 年 1 月 1 日及之后的；或在无合同交付日期的情况下，船舶设备的实际交付日期在 2029 年 1 月 1 日及之后。

4. 申明需持续审查航线改变功能的使用情况，并制定供本组织通过的相关操作指南。

5. 敦促各缔约国政府提醒有关航行安全和海上交通效率的各相关方：

（a）考虑仅将船—岸与岸—船航线交换视为基本意图指示。

（b）根据《SOLAS 公约》第 V/34 条和 V/34-1 条，必须始终尊重船长的酌处权；和

6. 撤销 MSC.530（106）号决议。

附 件

电子海图显示和信息系统（ECDIS）性能标准

1 ECDIS 的范围

1.1 ECDIS 的主要功能是保障航行安全。

1.2 配备适当备用系统的 ECDIS 可视为符合 1974 年《SOLAS 公约》第 V/19 条和 V/27 条对于最新海图和航海出版物的要求。在本文件中，电子航行数据服务（ENDS）的定义涵盖《SOLAS 公约》第 V 章和现行 IHO 标准中定义的海图和航海出版物。

1.3 ECDIS 应能显示保障安全和高效航行所需的所有航海信息，包括由政府、授权海道测量机构或其他相关政府机构制定和发布或核准的数据，以满足《SOLAS 公约》第 V/19 条和 V/27 条的要求。

1.4 ECDIS 应支持简单、可靠的 ENDS 数据更新。

1.5 与使用纸质海图和航海出版物相比，ECDIS 应减轻航行工作负担，使航海人员能以简便和及时的方式执行所有航线计划、航线监控和定位工作。系统应能持续指示、监控并记录船舶位置。

1.6 ECDIS 显示屏还可用于叠加显示雷达、雷达跟踪目标信息、AIS 和其他相关数据层，以辅助航线监控。

1.7 ECDIS 应针对信息显示或设备故障提供适当的警报或指示（见附录 5），并符合《驾驶台警报管理性能标准》[MSC.302（87）号决议]的要求。

1.8 如相关海图信息无法以适当格式（见第 4 节）获取，部分 ECDIS 设备可按照附录 7 的指引在栅格海图显示系统（RCDS）模式下运行。RCDS 操作模式应符合不低于附录 7 规定的性能标准。

2 本标准的适用范围

2.1 本性能标准适用于所有船舶配备的 ECDIS 设备，包括：
（1）专用独立工作站；和
（2）作为惯性导航系统（INS）组成部分的多功能工作站。

2.2 本性能标准适用于 ECDIS 操作模式、附录 7 规定的 RCDS 操作模式下的 ECDIS 和附录 6 规定的 ECDIS 备用系统配置要求。

2.3　ENDS 的结构、格式、加密显示要求属于相关 IHO 标准范畴，包括附录 1 中列出的标准。

2.4　除 A.694（17）号决议[①]中的通用要求和经修订的 MSC.191（79）号决议中显示的要求外，ECDIS 设备还应符合本标准的要求，并遵循本组织通过的人机工程学相关指南[②]。

3　定义

就本性能标准而言：

3.1　电子海图显示和信息系统（ECDIS）系指一种配备适当备用系统、遵循《SOLAS 公约》第 V/19 条和 V/27 条对最新海图和航海出版物要求的导航信息系统，可有选择地显示系统数据库信息及航行传感器的位置信息，帮助航海人员进行航线规划和航线监控，并可根据需求显示其他关于航行的信息。

3.2　电子海图（ENC）系指由政府、授权海道测量机构或其他相关政府机构发布的与 ECDIS 一起使用的数据库，其内容、结构和格式都已标准化，并符合 IHO 标准。ENC 包含安全航行所需的所有航海图信息。

3.3　电子航行数据服务（ENDS）系指使用航海图和航海出版物数据编制的专用数据库，由政府、授权海道测量机构或其他相关政府机构发布，与 ECDIS 一起使用，其内容、结构和格式都已标准化，并符合 IHO 标准；以及符合《SOLAS 公约》第 V/19 和 V/27 条对于航海、航海图和航海出版物的要求。ENDS 的导航基础层是 ENC。

3.4　系统数据库系指按照制造商内部 ECDIS 格式、由 ENDS 内容及其更新数据经无损转换后形成的一个数据库。ECDIS 通过访问该数据库实现海图显示并完成其他导航功能，该数据库等同于最新版 ENDS。

3.5　标准显示系指在航线规划和航线监控时至少应使用的显示模式，其海图内容列于附录 2。

3.6　基本显示系指附录 2 所列且不能从显示中移除的海图内容。基本显示不足以独立保障航行安全。

3.7　更多 ECDIS 定义详见 IHO 出版物 S-32《海道测量词典》（见附录 1）。

---

① 海安会 MSC/Circ.982 通函《驾驶台设备和布置的人机工程学衡准指南》。
② 参见 IEC 出版物 60945。

模块 A——数据库

4 提供和更新

4.1 ECDIS 所使用的 ENDS 信息应由政府、授权海道测量机构或其他相关政府机构发布，且符合列于附录 1 中的 IHO 标准。

4.2 系统数据库的内容应是完整和最新的，以使规划航程符合《SOLAS 公约》第 V/19 和 V/27 条的要求。

4.3 ENDS 或由 ENDS 转换的系统数据库信息不得被窜改。ENDS 内容的显示应符合 IHO 标准，包括互操作性规则。

4.4 ECDIS 应能接受符合 IHO 标准的官方 ENDS 更新，并自动应用于系统数据库。无论以何种方式进行更新，其执行过程不得干扰当前显示界面。

4.5 ECDIS 还应能接受手动输入的 ENDS 更新数据，并在最终接受数据前提供简单的验证方式。这些数据在显示时应同 ENDS 信息及其官方更新有区别，且不影响显示的清晰度。

4.6 ECDIS 应对各次更新（包括应用于系统数据库的时间）进行记录并在需要时显示记录。该记录应包括每个 ENDS 的各次更新历史，直至被新版替代。

4.7 ECDIS 应允许航海人员查阅各次更新记录，以审查其内容并核实其已被纳入系统数据库。

4.8 ECDIS 应能接收符合《IHO 数据保护方案》[①] 的 ENDS。

模块 B——操作和功能要求

5 系统数据库信息显示

5.1 ECDIS 应能接收和转换 ENDS 及其各次更新数据，并将其纳入系统数据库。ECDIS 应能显示和处理 IHO 规定的所有系统数据库信息。根据《IHO 决议》[②]，ECDIS 应能接受岸基转换生成的系统数据库。

5.2 可在航线规划和航线监控时显示的系统数据库信息应分为以下 3 种

[①] IHO 出版物 S-63《IHO 数据保护方案》（适用于 S-57ENCs），S-100 第 15 部分《数据保护方案》（适用于 S-100 产品）（见附录 1）。

[②] IHO 出版物 M-3《IHO 决议》。

类型：基本显示、标准显示和所有其他信息（见附录2）。

5.3 ECDIS应能通过单一操作随时切换至标准显示模式。

5.4 ECDIS在关闭或断电后重新启动时，应自动恢复至最近一次手动选择的显示设置。

5.5 ECDIS显示的信息应易于添加或移除，但不能移除基本显示中的信息。

5.6 对操作员确定的任何地理位置（例如通过光标选择），ECDIS应在需要时显示与该位置相关的海图要素信息。

5.7 应能通过适当的步骤（例如通过设置海图比例尺值或海里范围）改变显示画面的比例尺。

5.8 航海人员应能从系统数据库提供的信息中选择安全等深线。ECDIS应在显示的等深线中突出标示安全等深线。然而：

（1）如果航海人员未指定安全等深线，则默认为30米。如果航海人员指定的安全等深线或默认的30米等深线在系统数据库中不存在，则自动采用下一个较深的等深线；

（2）如因源数据改变导致当前安全等深线无法使用，应自动采用下一个较深的安全等深线；

（3）上述每种情况发生时，系统均应发出提示；和

（4）航海人员应能够选择永久显示安全等深线和安全水深设置。

5.9 航海人员应能选择设定一个安全水深值。当选择显示点水深时，ECDIS应突出显示等于或小于安全深度的水深值。

5.10 系统应支持动态水位调整，并发出提示。

5.11 ENDS及其所有更新数据的显示不得造成信息内容降级。

5.12 ECDIS应提供检验机制，确保ENDS及其所有更新数据已被正确地载入系统数据库。

5.13 ENDS数据及其更新内容应与其他显示信息明确区分，包括附录3所列信息。

6 比例尺

6.1 如遇下列情况，ECDIS应发出提示：
（1）信息显示比例大于ENC原始比例；
（2）本船位置存在比当前显示比例更大的ENC数据；或
（3）由于应用了最小显示比例，导致本船位置信息未显示。

7 其他航行信息的显示

7.1 可叠加显示符合本组织相关标准的雷达信息和/或 AIS 信息。其他航行信息可被添加到 ECDIS 显示中,但不应使系统数据库信息的显示降级,且必须与显示的系统数据库信息明确区分。

7.2 应能通过单一操作移除雷达信息、AIS 信息和其他导航信息。

7.3 ECDIS 和叠加的导航信息应使用统一的参考坐标系,否则系统应发出提示。

7.4 雷达:

7.4.1 传输的雷达信息可包含雷达图像和/或跟踪目标信息。

7.4.2 如将雷达图像叠加到 ECDIS 显示中,海图和雷达图像的比例尺、投影和方向应匹配。

7.4.3 雷达图像和位置传感器测得的位置数据应能自动调节天线与导航位置的偏移量。

8 显示模式和邻近区域的生成

8.1 系统数据库信息始终支持"北向上"的方向显示,并允许将其设置为其他方向。当设置为其他方向时,方位调整应按足够大的步幅改变,以避免海图信息显示不稳定。

8.2 ECDIS 应提供真实动态模式,及其他可选模式。

8.3 在使用真实动态模式时,邻近区域的海图显示应根据航海人员确定的本船与显示边缘的距离自动调整和生成。

8.4 应支持手动改变海图显示区域和本船相对于显示边缘的位置。

8.5 如果在 ECDIS 显示覆盖的区域中,一些水域没有可用于导航的合适比例尺的 ENC,这些水域应显示提示标志(见附录 5),提醒航海人员参考纸质海图或使用 RCDS 操作模式(见附录 7)。

9 颜色和符号

9.1 系统数据库信息应使用 IHO 推荐的颜色和符号标准[①]。

---

① IHO 出版物 S-52《海图内容和 ECDIS 显示规范》,S-101 中的《图式表达目录》(见附录 1)和 S-98 标准。

9.2 除9.1条所述的颜色和符号，其他颜色和符号应符合 IMO 导航符号标准中的适用要求[①]。

9.3 ECDIS 应允许航海人员选择以真实比例或符号形式显示本船。

10 显示要求

10.1 ECDIS 应能显示以下信息：
（1）航线规划和辅助导航任务；和
（2）航线监控。

10.2 航线监控所用海图显示的有效尺寸应至少为 270 毫米×270 毫米。

10.3 显示应符合 IHO 关于颜色和分辨率的推荐标准[②]。

10.4 显示方式应确保所显示的信息能使一名以上的观察员在船舶驾驶室正常灯光条件下在白天或晚上都可以清晰辨识。

10.5 如果在自定义显示内容时移除了标准显示中的信息类目（见附录2），应发出持续提示。在需要时应可显示从标准显示中移除的信息类目。

11 航线规划、调整、监控和航程记录

11.1 系统应能以简单、可靠的方法进行航线规划、航线监控和航线调整。

11.2 ECDIS 在船舶穿过其安全等深线和进入禁航区时发出的各种警报或提示（见附录5），应始终使用给定区域的系统数据库能够提供的最大比例尺数据。

11.3 航线规划及调整：

11.3.1 应支持制定包括直线段、曲线段和时间表的航线规划。

11.3.2 应支持用字符输入和图形界面操作调整航线规划，包括：
（1）在航线中增加航路点；
（2）从航线中删除航路点；和
（3）修改航路点的位置。

11.3.3 除了已选择的航线外，还应能规划一条或多条备选航线。已选择的航线应能与其他航线明确区分。

---

① SN. 1/Circ. 243/Rev. 2 通函。
② IHO 出版物 S-52《海图内容和 ECDIS 显示规范》，S-101 中的《图式表达目录》（见附录1）和 S-98 标准。

11.3.4 应能与岸基海事服务人员交流、发送和接收已选择和备选航线规划。传输应遵循航线规划传输的标准格式①，并应使用包括信息安全保护②在内的标准服务接口，以确保机对机通信安全。接收到的航线规划应被视为首选计划的基本指示，并应在 ECDIS 中明确显示仅作为航线规划使用。根据《SOLAS 公约》第 V/34 条和 V/34-1 条的要求，接收到的航线规划的使用应由船长控制，并尊重船长的专业判断和酌处权。

11.3.5 更改后的航线规划应有航线时间表，包括预计离港时间和预计到港时间，只要这些信息有一定准确性。

11.3.6 如果航海人员制定的航线规划与本船的安全等深线的距离小于用户设定的安全距离，应有图形提示。

11.3.7 如果航海人员制定的航线规划与用户可选类别的禁航区或有特殊条件的地理区域（见附录 4）边界的距离小于用户设定的安全距离，应有图形提示。如果航海人员制定的航线规划与用户可选类别的点目标（例如固定或浮动的航标或孤立危险物）的距离小于用户设定的安全距离，也应有图形提示。用户可选类别应与用户选择的显示目标相同并符合 IHO 标准。当取消用户可选类别时，应有持续提示。在需要时应可提供取消选项的详情。

11.3.8 根据 IHO 标准所定义的相关海道测量信息的精度信息，航海人员应能选择 11.3.6 和 11.3.7 的提示。

11.3.9 还应能根据 A.893（21）号决议的适用部分进行一次完整的航线检查，以支持评估和规划过程。检查发现的目标应以图形形式供复核，并在需要时以文本形式供检视。

11.3.10 航海人员应能规定偏离规划航线的偏航警报（即交叉航迹）阈值，并在达到此阈值时，自动启动偏航警报。

11.4 航线监控：

11.4.1 就航线监控而言，所选航线和本船位置只要在屏幕显示范围内就应持续显示。

11.4.2 在进行航线监控期间，应能显示船舶所在范围以外的海域（例如在查看前方、规划航线时）。如果该操作在航线监控的显示器上执行，那么航线自动监控功能（例如更新船舶位置、触发警报和提示）应保持持续运行。操作员应能通过单一操作立即返回到显示本船位置的航线监控界面。

11.4.3 航海人员应可设定时间或距离预警值，当本船驶近至距安全等深线小于该设定值的区域时，ECDIS 应发出警报并显示相关图形提示。取消设定

---

① IEC 61174/IEC 6317-1。

② IEC 63173-2。

安全等深线警报时，应有持续提示。

11.4.4 航海人员应可设定时间或距离预警值，当本船驶近至用户可选类别的禁航区或与特殊条件的地理区域（见附录4）的边界的距离小于用户设定值时，ECDIS应根据航海人员的选择发出警告、提醒或提示并显示相关图形提示。用户可选类别应与用户选择显示的物标相同并遵循IHO标准。当任何用户可选类别被禁用时，应有持续提示。在需要时应可提供禁用详情。

11.4.5 如果规划航线时航海人员设定了偏离选择航线的偏航警报阈值，当航线偏离超过阈值时，应发出警报。

11.4.6 如果本船按当前航向和航速继续航行，在航海人员设定的特定时间或距离内，本船将航经用户可选类别的浅于用户设定的安全等深线的危险物（例如障碍物、沉船、礁石）或航标，且小于用户设定的安全距离，则ECDIS应根据航海人员的设置发出警告、提醒或提示，并给出相关的图形提示。用户可选类别应与用户选择显示的物标相同，并遵循IHO标准。当任何用户可选类别被禁用时，应有持续提示。在需要时应可提供禁用详情。

11.4.7 如果当前或下一段航线与安全等深线的距离小于用户设定的安全距离时，应发出图形提示。

11.4.8 如果当前或下一段航线与用户可选类别的禁航区或有特殊条件的地理区域（见附录4）的边界的距离小于用户设定的安全距离，应发出图形提示。如果选择的航线与用户可选类别的点目标（例如固定或浮动的航标或孤立的危险物）的距离小于用户设定的安全距离，也应发出图形提示。用户可选类别应与用户选择显示的物标相同并遵循IHO标准。

11.4.9 航海者应能选择11.4.3、11.4.4、11.4.6、11.4.7和11.4.8条款的提示是否包含IHO标准所定义的相关海道测量信息的精度信息。

11.4.10 船只定位应来自连续定位系统，其精度应符合安全航行的要求。在可能的情况下，应配置第二个独立的且最好是不同类型的定位系统。在此情况下，ECDIS应能识别两个系统之间的差异。

11.4.11 当船只定位、航向或航速信号输入中断时，ECDIS应发出警告。ECDIS还应重复（但仅作为提示）从船只定位、航向或航速信号源传来的任何警报或提示。

11.4.12 当船舶到达距规划航线上航海人员设定的关键点预警时间或距离阈值时，ECDIS应发出警告。

11.4.13 定位系统和系统数据库应采用相同的地理坐标系，否则ECDIS应发出警告。

11.4.14 除已选择的航线之外，还应能显示备选航线。已选择的航线应与其他航线明确区分。在航行时，航海人员应能修改选择的航线或改用其他备选航线。

11.4.15 如果已选择的航线在航行过程中发生变化，应能将更新后的航线规划发送给岸基海事服务提供者。来自岸基海事服务人员的航线规划须经船长确认后方可用于航程监控。

11.4.16 应支持显示以下信息：

（1）船舶航迹时间标签（可手动显示或在 1 分钟到 120 分钟之间设定时间间隔自动显示）；和

（2）足够数量的点、可自由移动的电子方位线、可变/固定的范围标志，以及附录 3 中指定的导航所需的其他符号。

11.4.17 应能输入任何位置的地理坐标，并根据需要显示该位置。此外，还应能选择显示的任何点（要素、符号或位置），并根据需要读取其地理坐标。

11.4.18 应能手动调整显示的船舶地理位置。该手动调整应以字符数字的形式显示在屏幕上，在航海人员更改前保持不变，并自动记录。

11.4.19 ECDIS 应支持输入和标绘人工获得的方位线和距离位置线（LOP），并推算本船的位置。推算出的船只位置应能作为航位推算的原点。

11.4.20 ECDIS 应显示持续定位系统获得的位置和人工观测获得的位置之间的差异。

11.5 航程记录：

11.5.1 ECDIS 应支持存储并重建航行所需的某些最小元素，以及验证过去 12 小时使用的官方数据库。下列数据应每分钟记录一次：

（1）本船的历史航迹：时间、船位、航向和航速；

（2）使用过的官方数据记录：ENC 数据来源、版本、日期、单元和更新历史；

（3）对安全等深线、预测和航线监控警报设置的任何改变。

11.5.2 ECDIS 应将 11.5.1（2）条和 11.5.1（3）条中所列的信息输出到航行数据记录仪。

11.5.3 另外，ECDIS 应对全航程进行完整的航迹记录，时间标记间隔不超过 4 小时。

11.5.4 不得对已记录的信息进行窜改。

11.5.5 ECDIS 应具备保存过去 12 小时记录以及历史航迹的功能。

12 计算和精度

12.1 ECDIS 中所有计算的精度应不受输出装置特性的影响，并与系统数据库的精度保持一致。

12.2 显示中所绘的方位和距离,或显示中已有的要素之间测得的方位和距离的精度,应不低于显示分辨率的精度。

12.3 该系统至少应能运行并显示下列计算及其结果:
(1) 两个地理位置之间的真实距离和方位;
(2) 已知位置结合距离和方位的地理位置;
(3) 地理测量计算,例如球面距离、恒向线和大圆。

13 性能测试、故障警报和提示

13.1 ECDIS 应配备针对主要功能的自动或手动进行的船上测试。如发生故障,测试应显示故障模块信息。

13.2 当系统发生故障时,ECDIS 应发出适当的警告或提示。

14 备用系统配置

应配备足够的备用系统配置,以保证在 ECDIS 发生故障时的航行安全(见附录6)。

(1) 应有安全取代 ECDIS 功能的设施,防止 ECDIS 故障演变为危急情况。
(2) 备用系统配置应在 ECDIS 发生故障的情况下,为剩余航程提供安全航行指引。

模块 C——接口和集成

15 外部设备连接[①]

15.1 ECDIS 不应降低任何传感输入设备的性能,也不应因连接可选设备而使 ECDIS 的性能低于本标准。

15.2 ECDIS 应连接船舶定位系统、电罗经及测速测距仪。对于未配备电罗经的船舶,ECDIS 应连接船用发射航向装置。

15.3 ECDIS 应具备向外部设备提供系统数据库信息的功能。

---

① 出版物 IEC 61162。

16　电力供应

16.1　根据《SOLAS 公约》第Ⅱ-1 章有关要求，ECDIS 及正常运行所需设备应能由应急电源供电。

16.2　电源切换或供电中断不超过 45 秒时，设备应不需要手动重新启动。

附录 1

参考文件

以下国际组织已制定了与本标准配套使用的技术标准和规范。这些资料的最新版本可向相关组织索取。

国际海事组织(IMO)

地址：国际海事组织
      4 Albert Embankment
      伦敦 SE1 7SR
      英国

电话：+44 207 735 76 11
传真：+44 207 587 32 10
电子邮箱：info@imo.org
网址：http://www.imo.org

出版物

经 MSC.466（101）号决议修订的 MSC.191（79）号决议《关于船载航行显示器航行信息的显示性能标准》

A.694（17）号决议《关于全球海上遇险和安全系统（GMDSS）船载无线电设备和电子导航设备的通用要求建议案》

MSC.302（87）号决议《驾驶台警报管理性能标准》

MSC.1/Circ.1503/Rev.2 号通函《ECDIS 良好实践指南》

SN.1/Circ.243/Rev.2 号通函《与航行有关的符号、术语和缩写的显示指南》

MSC/Circ.982 号通函《驾驶台设备和布置的人机工程学衡准指南》

国际海道测量组织 (IHO)

地址：指导委员会
      国际海道测量组织
      BP 445
      MC 98011 Monaco Cedex
      摩纳哥国

电话：+377 93 10 81 00
传真：+377 93 10 81 40
电子邮箱：info@iho.int
网址：http://www.iho.int

出版物

IHO 出版物 S-52《海图内容和 ECDIS 显示规范》
IHO 出版物 S-52 附录 1《电子海图更新导则》
IHO 出版物 S-52 附录 2《ECDIS 颜色和符号规范》
IHO 出版物 S-32《海道测量词典》
IHO 出版物 S-57《IHO 海道测量数据传输标准》
IHO 出版物 S-100《IHO 通用海道测量数据模型》
IHO 出版物 S-101《电子海图（ENC）产品规范》
IHO 出版物 S-98《S-100 导航系统中的数据产品互操作》
IHO 出版物 S-61《IHO 栅格海图（RNC）产品规范》
IHO 出版物 S-63《IHO 数据保护方案》
IHO 出版物 M-3《IHO 决议》
https://iho.int/en/standards-in-force

国际电工委员会（IEC）

地址：IEC 总办公室
3 rue de Varemb
PO Box 131
CH-1211 Geneva 20
瑞士

电话：+41 22 919 02 11
电子邮箱：info@iec.ch
网站：www.iec.ch

出版物

IEC 出版物 61174《电子海图显示和信息系统（ECDIS）操作和性能要求、测试方法和测试结果要求》

IEC 出版物 60945《全球海上遇险和安全系统船载无线电设备和电子导航设备的通用要求》

IEC 出版物 61162《数字接口——船上导航和无线电通信设备》

IEC 出版物 62288《海上导航和无线电通信设备及系统 导航相关信息的显示、通用要求、测试方法和测试结果要求》

IEC 出版物 63173-1《海上导航和无线电通信设备及系统 数字接口 第一部分：基于 S-100 的 S-421 航线规划》

附录 1　参考文件

IEC 出版物 63173-2《海上导航和无线电通信设备及系统 数字接口 第二部分：船岸之间的安全通信》

附录 2

可用于航线规划和航线监控显示的系统数据库信息

1 永久显示于 ECDIS 显示器上的基础显示,包括:
(1) 海岸线(高水位);
(2) 本船的安全等深线;
(3) 位于安全等深线所界定的安全水域内,且深度小于安全等深线的水下孤立危险物;
(4) 位于安全等深线所界定的安全水域内的孤立危险物,例如固定构筑物、架空电缆等;
(5) 比例尺、范围和指北针;
(6) 水深和高度单位;
(7) 显示模式。

2 标准显示包括:
(1) 基础显示;
(2) 干出线;
(3) 浮标、灯塔、其他航标和固定构筑物;
(4) 航道、海峡等边界;
(5) 目视和雷达显著物标;
(6) 禁航区和限航区;
(7) 海图比例尺边界;
(8) 警示语句的提示;
(9) 船舶定线制和渡轮航线;
(10) 群岛海上航路。

3 根据需要,其他信息可单独显示,例如:
(1) 水深点;
(2) 海底电缆和管道;
(3) 所有孤立危险物的详细信息;
(4) 航标的详细信息;
(5) 警示语句的内容;
(6) ENC 版本日期;
(7) 最近海图更新号;

附录 2　可用于航线规划和航线监控显示的系统数据库信息

（8）磁差；
（9）经纬线；
（10）地名。

附录 3

导航要素和参数

1 本船：
（1）主要航线的历史航迹（含时间标记）。
（2）次要航线的历史航迹（含时间标记）。
2 实际航向和航速的矢量线。
3 可变距离标志和/或电子方位线。
4 光标。
5 事件标记：
（1）推算船位和时间（DR）。
（2）估计船位和时间（EP）。
6 定位点和时间。
7 位置线和时间。
8 移动的位置线和时间。
9 潮汐数据：
（1）预报的潮流或海流矢量及其有效时间和流速。
（2）计算的潮流或海流矢量及其有效时间和流速。
10 高亮显示的危险物。
11 避险线。
12 计划最佳航向和航速。
13 航路点。
14 航行距离。
15 有日期和时间的计划船位。
16 转向点位置和时间。

附录 4

有特殊条件的区域

ECDIS 按照第 11.3.7 条和 11.4.4 条要求，对下列区域进行检测并发出警报或提示：

分道通航区
沿岸通航区
限制区
警戒区
近海生产区
避航区
用户自定义的避航区
军事演习区
水上飞机降落区
潜水艇通道
锚（泊）地
渔场/水产养殖区
特殊敏感海域（PSSA）

附录 5

警报和提示标识

表 1　警报和提示的意义

段落	要求	信息
11.4.3	警报	与安全等深线的距离小于设定的距离
11.4.4	警告/提醒/提示	与有特殊条件的区域的距离小于设定的距离
11.4.5	警报	偏离航线
11.4.6	警告/提醒/提示	以航线监控模式通过危险物的距离小于设定的距离
11.4.11	警告	定位系统发生故障
11.4.12	警告	接近临界点
11.4.13	警告	不同的地理坐标系
13.2	警告/提示	ECDIS 系统故障
5.8（3）	提示	默认安全等深线
6.1（1）	提示	信息显示比例尺超过规定比例尺
6.1（2）	提示	存在比例尺更大的 ENC
6.1（3）	提示	由于使用最小比例尺，信息不能显示
7.3	提示	不同的参考系统
8.5	提示	无可用的 ENC 数据
10.5	提示	自定义显示
11.3.6	提示	航线规划与安全等深线的距离小于设定的距离
11.3.7	提示	航线规划与指定区域的距离小于设定的距离
11.4.7	提示	监控航线与安全等深线的距离小于设定的距离
11.4.8	提示	监控航线与指定区域或危险物的距离小于设定的距离
13.1	提示	系统检测失败

在本性能标准中，A.1021（26）号决议《警报和提示代码》（2009）和 MSC.302（87）号决议《驾驶台警报管理性能标准》中规定的提示和警报的定义适用。

附录5 警报器和提示器

警报：对于需要注意的状况发出的听觉和/或视觉信息。警报按优先顺序分为警报、警告和提醒。

提示：发出关于系统或设备状况信息的视觉提示。

附录 6

备用系统配置要求

1 引言

本性能标准第 14 节规定,应有足够的独立备用系统,以确保当 ECDIS 发生故障时的航行安全。具体安排包括:

(1) 具备安全取代 ECDIS 功能的设施,以确保 ECDIS 故障不会引发危急情况;和

(2) 当 ECDIS 发生故障时,保障余下航程能安全航行的手段。

2 目的

ECDIS 备用系统的目的是确保当 ECDIS 发生故障时,不会危及航行安全。这应包括在各种危急航行情况下及时切换至备用系统。备用系统应支持船舶安全航行直至航程结束。

3 功能要求

3.1 必备功能及其有效性

3.1.1 海图信息的显示

备用系统应以图形(海图)形式显示安全航行所需的海道测量和地理环境相关信息。

3.1.2 航线规划

备用系统应具备航线规划的功能,包括:

(1) 接管原本在 ECDIS 上执行的航线规划;

(2) 手动或通过航线规划设备传输航线。

3.1.3 航线监控

备用系统应能接管原本由 ECDIS 进行的航线监控,并至少提供下列功能:

(1) 自动获取或在海图上手动标绘本船的位置;

(2) 从海图获得航向、距离和方位信息;

(3) 显示规划航线;

(4) 航迹线时间标记；
(5) 在海图上标绘足够数量的点、方位线、距离标记等。

3.1.4 信息显示

如果备用系统是电子设备，它应能显示至少等同于本性能标准所定义的标准显示的信息。

3.1.5 海图信息的提供

(1) 备用系统使用的海图信息应为政府、授权海道测量机构或其他相关政府机构发布并经官方更新的最新版本，且符合 IHO 标准。
(2) 禁止窜改电子海图的内容。
(3) 应明确标注海图或海图数据的版本和发布日期。

3.1.6 更新

ECDIS 备用系统显示的信息应包括整个航程中的最新信息。

3.1.7 比例尺

如使用电子设备，应在下列情况下发出提示：
(1) 信息以比数据库中的比例尺更大的比例尺显示；
(2) 海图以比系统提供的比例尺更大的比例尺显示本船的位置。

3.1.8 如果在备用电子显示系统中叠加雷达和其他航行信息，应满足本性能标准对雷达信息和其他航行信息的所有相关要求。

3.1.9 如使用电子设备，邻近区域的显示模式和生成应符合本性能标准第 8 节。

3.1.10 航程记录

备用系统应能保持对船舶实际航迹的记录，包括船舶位置和对应时间。

3.2 可靠性和精度

3.2.1 可靠性

备用系统应能在主要环境条件和正常操作条件下稳定运行。

3.2.2 精度

精度应符合本性能标准第 12 节的要求。

3.3 故障、警报和提示

如使用电子设备，应提供系统故障的适当警告或提示。

4 操作要求

4.1 人机工程学

如使用电子设备，电子设备应按 ECDIS 人机工程学原理设计。

4.2　信息显示

如果使用电子设备：

（1）颜色和符号应符合 ECDIS 对颜色和符号的要求；和

（2）海图显示的有效尺寸应不小于 270 毫米×270 毫米或 270 毫米的直径。

5　电力供应

如果使用电子设备：

（1）备用电源应独立于 ECDIS 系统；和

（2）应符合 ECDIS 性能标准的要求。

6　外部设备连接

6.1　如果使用电子设备，应：

（1）与船舶定位系统、电罗经、测速测距仪连接。对于没有配置电罗经的船舶，ECDIS 应连接船用传送航向装置；

（2）不得降低任何传感输入设备的性能。

6.2　如果包含被选定 ENC 海图信息覆盖范围的雷达被用作备用系统的一部分，该雷达应符合 MSC.192（79）号决议。

附录7

栅格海图显示系统（RCDS）操作模式

本附录中凡提到有关 ECDIS 的内容，应视具体情况以栅格海图显示系统（RCDS）替换 ECDIS，以系统栅格海图数据库（SRNC）替换系统数据库，以栅格海图（RNC）替换电子海图（ENC）。

本附录与 ECDIS 性能标准（即本标准，本部分是其附录7）的段落相对应，并标明本附录中的具体段落为以下情况之一：

(1) 适用于 RCDS；或

(2) 不适用于 RCDS；或

(3) 已按说明被调整或替代以适用于 RCDS，并对适用于 RCDS 的任何附加要求进行了说明。

1 范围

1.1 适用于 RCDS。

1.2 当以 RCDS 模式运行时，船上应配备合适的最新纸质海图文件包（APC），供航海人员随时取用。

1.3—1.6 适用于 RCDS。

1.7 RCDS 应对显示信息或设备故障发出适当的警报或提示（见本附录表1）。

1.8 参见附录7且适用于 RCDS。

2 本标准的适用范围

2.1—2.4 适用于 RCDS。

3 定义

3.1 栅格海图显示系统（RCDS）系指一种航行信息系统，它通过来自航行传感器的位置信息显示 RNC，帮助航海人员进行航线规划和航线监控，有需要时，还可以显示其他关于航行的信息。

3.2 栅格海图（RNC）系指政府授权海道测量机构制作或发布的纸质海

图的复制品。本标准中使用的 RNC 可指单张海图，也可指海图合集。

3.3 不适用于 RCDS。

3.4 系统栅格海图数据库（SRNC）系指经 RCDS 转换的 RNC 数据库（含官方更新）。

3.5—3.6 不适用于 RCDS。

3.7 适用于 RCDS。

3.8 适用的最新纸质海图文件包（APC）系指一套纸质海图，以合适的比例尺详细显示地形、水深、危险碍航物、航标、航线以及定线制，向航海人员提供综合的航行环境信息。APC 应具备充分掌握前方航行区信息的能力。沿岸国会提供满足该文件包要求的海图详细信息，这些详细信息已被纳入由 IHO 维护的全球数据库。确定 APC 内容时应考虑该数据库中包含的详细信息。

模块 A——数据库

4 海图信息的提供和更新

4.1 RCDS 中使用的 RNC 应为政府授权海道测量机构制定或发布的 RNC 的最新版本，并符合 IHO 标准。非基于 WGS 84 或 PE-90 的 RNC 应附带元数据（即附加数据），使地理参考定位数据能按与 SRNC 数据的正确关系显示。

4.2 SRNC 的内容应覆盖 ENC 未包含的航段且保持更新。

4.3 禁止修改 RNC 的内容。

4.4—4.7 均适用于 RCDS。

4.8 不适用于 RCDS。

模块 B——操作和功能要求

5 SRNC 信息的显示

5.1 RCDS 应能显示所有 SRNC 信息。

5.2 航线规划和航线监控期间，可供显示的 SRNC 信息应分为 2 类：

（1）由 RNC 及其各次更新组成的 RCDS 标准显示，包括其比例尺、显示比例尺、水平基准及其深度和高度单位；

（2）任何其他信息，例如航海人员注意事项。

5.3—5.4 适用于 RCDS。

5.5 RCDS 显示应易于添加或移除 RNC 数据以外的任何附加信息，例如航海人员注意事项。禁止删除 RNC 信息。

5.6—5.10 不适用于 RCDS。

5.11 适用于 RCDS。

5.12 RCDS 应提供措施确保 RNC 及其所有更新正确载入系统。

5.13 RCDS 及其所有更新应与显示的其他信息明确区分,包括附录 3 所列内容。

5.14 如果 ECDIS 设备正以 RCDS 模式操作,应持续提示。

6 比例尺

本节内容均适用于 RCDS。

7 其他航行信息的显示

7.1—7.4 均适用于 RCDS。

8 显示模式和邻近区域的生成

8.1 应始终能以"海图朝上"方向显示 SRNC,并允许以其他方向显示。

8.2—8.4 均适用于 RCDS。

8.5 参见 RCDS 操作模式。

9 颜色和符号

9.1 应使用 IHO 建议的颜色和符号描绘 SRNC 信息。

9.2 适用于 RCDS。

9.3 适用于 RCDS。

10 显示要求

10.1—10.2 适用于 RCDS。

10.3 不适用于 RCDS。

10.4 适用于 RCDS。

10.5 不适用于 RCDS。

10.6 RCDS 应能简单、快速地显示不在当前显示海图范围内的海图注记。

11 航线规划、调整、监控和航程记录

11.1 适用于 RCDS。

11.2 不适用于 RCDS。

11.3 航线规划

11.3.1—11.3.5 适用于 RCDS。

11.3.6—11.3.9 不适用于 RCDS。

11.3.10 适用于 RCDS。

11.4 航线监控

11.4.1 适用于 RCDS。

11.4.2 在进行航线监控时，应能显示船舶所在范围以外的海域（例如在查看前方、航线规划时）。如果这一操作是在航线监控的显示器上进行的，那么 11.4.11 条和 11.4.12 条所述的航线自动监控功能应是持续的。操作员应能通过单一操作立即恢复到覆盖本船位置的航线监控显示。

11.4.3—11.4.4 不适用于 RCDS。

11.4.5 适用于 RCDS。

11.4.6—11.4.9 不适用于 RCDS。

11.4.10—11.4.12 适用于 RCDS。

11.4.13 RCDS 应只接受参照 WGS 84 或 PE-90 大地基准面的位置数据。如果位置数据不参照这两个大地基准面，RCDS 应发出警告。如果显示的 RNC 不能参照 WGS 84 或 PE-90 大地基准面，应发出持续提示。

11.4.14—11.4.18 适用于 RCDS。

11.4.19 RCDS 应允许用户手动校准 SRNC 与位置数据对齐。这可能是必要的，例如可修正补偿局部海图误差。

11.4.20 当船舶穿过一个点或一条线，或在设定的时间或距离内进入航海人员输入的边界内时，应能触发自动警告。

11.5 航程记录

11.5.1—11.5.4 均适用于 RCDS。

12 计算和精度

12.1—12.3 均适用于 RCDS。

12.4 RCDS 应能在本地基准面和 WGS 84 基准面之间转换。

13 性能测试、故障警报和提示

13.1—13.2 均适用于 RCDS。

14 备用系统配置

本节内容均适用于 RCDS。

模块 C——接口和集成

15 外部设备连接

15.1—15.3 均适用于 RCDS。

16 电力供应

16.1—16.2 均适用于 RCDS。

表1 RCDS 操作模式的警报和提示

段落	要求	信息
11.4.5	警报	偏离航线
11.4.20	警告	接近航海人员输入的要素，例如区域、航线
11.4.11	警告	定位系统故障
11.4.12	警告	接近临界点
11.4.13	警告或提示	不同的大地基准面
13.2	警告或提示	RCDS 模式故障
5.13	提示	ECDIS 以栅格模式操作
6.1	提示	有可用的较大比例尺信息，或超过比例尺
6.1（2）	提示	船舶区域有可用的较大比例尺 RNC

注：警报和提示的定义见附录5。

RESOLUTION MSC. 530(106)/REV. 1
(adopted on 24 May 2024)

PERFORMANCE STANDARDS FOR ELECTRONIC CHART DISPLAY AND INFORMATION SYSTEMS (ECDIS)

THE MARITIME SAFETY COMMITTEE,

RECALLING Article 28(b) of the Convention on the International Maritime Organization concerning the functions of the Committee,

RECALLING ALSO resolution A. 886(21), by which the Assembly resolved that the function of adopting performance standards and technical specifications, as well as amendments thereto, shall be performed by the Maritime Safety Committee and/or the Marine Environment Protection Committee, as appropriate, on behalf of the Organization,

RECALLING FURTHER regulations V/19 and V/27 of the International Convention for the Safety of Life at Sea (SOLAS), 1974, which require all ships to carry adequate and up-to-date charts, sailing directions, lists of lights, notices to mariners, tide tables and all other nautical publications necessary for the intended voyage,

RECALLING resolutions A. 817(19), as amended, and MSC. 232(82), which have provided performance standards for electronic chart display and information systems (ECDIS),

NOTING that the up-to-date charts required by SOLAS regulations V/19 and V/27 can be provided and displayed electronically on board ships by ECDIS, and that the other nautical publications required by regulation V/27 may also be so provided and displayed,

NOTING ALSO the recent developments and enhancement of ECDIS, including new electronic navigational chart transfer functionality in the performance standards, are the necessary step towards the implementation of the e-navigation concept of harmonized Maritime Services,

RECALLING that, recognizing the need to improve the revised performance

PERFORMANCE STANDARDS FOR ELECTRONIC CHART DISPLAY AND INFORMATION SYSTEMS (ECDIS)

standards for ECDIS, previously adopted by resolution MSC.232(82), in order to ensure the operational reliability of such equipment and, taking into account the technological progress and experience gained, it had adopted resolution MSC.530 (106), which introduced the next technical generation of IHO standards of S-100 series,

RECOGNIZING the benefit in further enhancing the performance standards, by facilitating a standardized digital exchange of ships' route plans,

RECALLING that operational guidance on the ship-shore and shore-ship exchange of static and dynamic voyage information in the context of shipboard automatic identification systems (AIS) has been adopted by the Organization,

HAVING CONSIDERED the recommendation made by the Sub-Committee on Navigation, Communications and Search and Rescue, at its tenth session,

1 ADOPTS the revised performance standards for electronic chart display and information systems (ECDIS), set out in the annex to the present resolution;

2 RECOMMENDS Governments to ensure that ECDIS equipment:

(a) if installed on or after 1 January 2029, conforms to performance standards not inferior to those specified in the annex to the present resolution;

(b) if installed on or after 1 January 2026 but before 1 January 2029, conforms either to performance standards not inferior to those specified in the annex to the present resolution or to performance standards not inferior to those specified in the annex to resolution MSC.232(82);

(c) if installed on or after 1 January 2009 but before 1 January 2026, conforms to performance standards not inferior to those specified in the annex to resolution MSC.232(82); and

(d) if installed on or after 1 January 1996 but before 1 January 2009, conforms to performance standards not inferior to those specified in the annex to resolution A.817(19), as amended by resolutions MSC.64(67) and MSC.86(70);

3 AGREES that, for the purpose of this resolution, the expression *installed on or after 1 January 2029* means:

(a) for ships for which the building contract is placed on or after 1 January 2029, or in the absence of the contract, constructed on or after 1 January 2029, any installation date on the ship; or

(b) for ships other than those prescribed in (a) above, a contractual delivery date for the equipment or, in the absence of a contractual delivery date, the actual delivery date of the equipment to the ship on or after 1 January 2029;

4   AFFIRMS the need to keep the use of route exchange under review and to develop appropriate operational guidance to be adopted by the Organization;

5   URGES Contracting Governments to remind all stakeholders in safety of navigation and efficiency of maritime traffic:

(a) to consider routes exchanged between ship-shore and shore-ship as a basic indication of intent only; and

(b) that the master's discretion must always be respected, in accordance with SOLAS regulations V/34 and V/34-1; and

6   REVOKES resolution MSC.530(106).

ANNEX

PERFORMANCE STANDARDS FOR ELECTRONIC CHART DISPLAY AND INFORMATION SYSTEMS (ECDIS)

1 SCOPE OF ECDIS

1.1 The primary function of ECDIS is to contribute to safe navigation.

1.2 ECDIS with adequate backup arrangements may be accepted as complying with the up-to-date charts and nautical publications required by regulations V/19 and V/27 of the 1974 SOLAS Convention. For the purpose of this document, the definition of electronic navigational data service (ENDS) encompasses the nautical charts and nautical publications as defined in SOLAS chapter V and IHO standards in force.

1.3 ECDIS should be capable of displaying all nautical information necessary for safe and efficient navigation, originated and distributed by or on the authority of a government, authorized hydrographic office or other relevant government institution, as required by SOLAS regulations V/19 and V/27.

1.4 ECDIS should facilitate simple and reliable updating of the ENDS.

1.5 ECDIS should reduce the navigational workload compared to using the paper chart and paper nautical publications. It should enable the mariner to execute in a convenient and timely manner all route planning, route monitoring and positioning. It should be capable of continuously indicating, monitoring and recording the ship's position.

1.6 The ECDIS display may also be used for the display of radar, radar tracked target information, AIS and other appropriate data layers to assist in route monitoring.

1.7 ECDIS should provide appropriate alerts or indications with respect to the information displayed or malfunction of the equipment (see appendix 5). ECDIS should meet the requirements of the *Performance standards for bridge alert management* [resolution MSC. 302(87)].

1.8　When the relevant chart information is not available in the appropriate form (see section 4), some ECDIS equipment may operate in the raster chart display system (RCDS) mode as defined in appendix 7. RCDS mode of operation should conform to performance standards not inferior to those set out in appendix 7.

2　APPLICATION OF THESE STANDARDS

2.1　These performance standards should apply to all ECDIS equipment carried on all ships, as follows:

(1) dedicated stand-alone workstation; and

(2) a multifunction workstation as part of an INS.

2.2　These performance standards apply to ECDIS mode of operation, ECDIS in RCDS mode of operation as specified in appendix 7 and ECDIS backup arrangements as specified in appendix 6.

2.3 Requirements for structure, format, encryption presentation of the ENDS are within the scope of relevant IHO standards, including those listed in appendix 1.

2.4　In addition to the general requirements set out in resolution A.694(17)① and the presentation requirements set out in resolution MSC.191(79), as amended, ECDIS equipment should meet the requirements of these standards and follow the relevant guidelines on ergonomic principles adopted by the Organization.②

3　DEFINITIONS

For the purpose of these performance standards:

3.1　Electronic chart display and information system (ECDlS) means a navigation information system which with adequate backup arrangements can be accepted as complying with the up-to-date nautical chart and nautical publications required by SOLAS regulations V/19 and V/27, by displaying selected information from a system database with positional information from navigation sensors to assist the mariner in route planning and route monitoring and, if required, display additional navigation-related information.

3.2　Electronic navigational chart (ENC) means the database, standardized

---

① MSC/Circ.982 on *Guidelines on ergonomic criteria for bridge equipment and layout*.
② Refer to Publication IEC 60945.

ANNEX PERFORMANCE STANDARDS FOR ELECTRONIC CHART DISPLAY AND INFORMATION SYSTEMS (ECDIS)

as to content, structure and format, issued for use with ECDIS by or on the authority of a government, authorized hydrographic office or other relevant government institution, and conforming to IHO standards. The ENC contains all the nautical chart information necessary for safe navigation.

3.3 Electronic navigational data service (ENDS) means a special-purpose database compiled from nautical chart and nautical publication data, standardized as to content, structure and format, issued for use with ECDIS by or on the authority of a government, authorized hydrographic office or other relevant government institution, and conforming to IHO standards; and which is designed to meet the requirement of marine navigation and the nautical charts and nautical publications carriage requirements in SOLAS regulations V/19 and V/27. The navigational base layer of ENDS is the electronic navigational chart (ENC).

3.4 System database means a database, in the manufacturer's internal ECDIS format, resulting from the lossless transformation of the ENDS contents and its updates. It is this database that is accessed by ECDIS for the display generation and other navigational functions, and is equivalent to up-to-date ENDS.

3.5 Standard display is the display mode intended to be used as a minimum during route planning and route monitoring. The chart content is listed in appendix 2.

3.6 *Display base* means the chart content as listed in appendix 2 and which cannot be removed from the display. It is not intended to be sufficient for safe navigation.

3.7 Further information on ECDIS definitions may be found in IHO Hydrographic Dictionary Publication S-32 (see appendix 1).

MODULE A—DATABASE

4 PROVISION AND UPDATING

4.1 The ENDS information to be used in ECDIS should be issued by or on the authority of a government, government-authorized hydrographic office or other relevant government institution, and conform to IHO standards as listed in appendix 1.

4.2 The contents of the system database should be adequate and up to date for the intended voyage to comply with SOLAS regulations V/19 and V/27.

4.3 It should not be possible to alter the contents of the ENDS or system database information transformed from the ENDS. The display of the content of ENDS should be compliant with IHO standards including rules set for interoperability.

4.4 ECDIS should be capable of accepting official updates to the ENDS provided in conformity with IHO standards. These updates should be automatically applied to the system database. By whatever means updates are received, the implementation procedure should not interfere with the display in use.

4.5 ECDIS should also be capable of accepting updates to the ENDS data entered manually with simple means for verification prior to the final acceptance of the data. They should be distinguishable on the display from ENDS information and its official updates and not affect display legibility.

4.6 ECDIS should keep and display on demand a record of updates including time of application to the system database. This record should include updates for each ENDS until it is superseded by a new edition.

4.7 ECDIS should allow the mariner to display updates in order to review their contents and to ascertain that they have been included in the system database.

4.8 ECDIS should be capable of accepting ENDS in accordance with the IHO Data Protection Scheme. ①

MODULE B—OPERATIONAL AND FUNCTIONAL REQUIREMENTS

5 DISPLAY OF SYSTEM DATABASE INFORMATION

5.1 An ECDIS should be capable of accepting and converting an ENDS and their updates into a system database. ECDIS should be capable of displaying and processing all system database information as specified by IHO. The ECDIS may also be capable of accepting a system database resulting from conversion ashore, in accordance with IHO resolutions. ②

5.2 System database information available for display during route planning and route monitoring should be subdivided into the following three categories: display

---

① IHO Publication S-63—Data Protection Scheme (for S-57 ENCs) and S-100, Part 15—Data Protection Scheme (for S-100 products) (see appendix 1).

② IHO Publication M-3—Resolutions of the IHO.

ANNEX PERFORMANCE STANDARDS FOR ELECTRONIC CHART DISPLAY AND INFORMATION SYSTEMS (ECDIS)

base, standard display and all other information (see appendix 2).

5.3 ECDIS should present the standard display at any time by a single operator action.

5.4 When an ECDIS is switched on following a switch off or power failure, it should return to the most recent manually selected settings for display.

5.5 It should be easy to add or remove information from the ECDIS display. It should not be possible to remove information contained in the display base.

5.6 For any operator-identified geographical position (e.g. by cursor picking), ECDIS should display on demand the information about the chart objects associated with such a position.

5.7 It should be possible to change the display scale by appropriate steps, e.g. by means of either chart scale values or ranges in nautical miles.

5.8 It should be possible for the mariner to select a safety contour from the information provided by the system database. ECDIS should emphasize the safety contour over other contours on the display. However:

(1) if the mariner does not specify a safety contour, this should default to 30 m. If the safety contour specified by the mariner or the default 30 m contour is not in the displayed system database, the safety contour shown should default to the next deeper contour;

(2) if the safety contour in use becomes unavailable owing to a change in source data, the safety contour should default to the next deeper contour;

(3) in each of the above cases, an indication should be provided; and

(4) the mariner should be able to select a permanent display of safety contour and safety depth settings.

5.9 It should be possible for the mariner to select a safety depth. ECDIS should emphasize soundings equal to or less than the safety depth whenever spot soundings are selected for display.

5.10 It should be possible to use dynamic water level adjustment and an indication should be provided.

5.11 The ENDS and all updates to it should be displayed without any degradation of their information content.

5.12 ECDIS should provide a means to ensure that the ENDS and all updates to it have been correctly loaded into the system database.

5.13 The ENDS data and updates to it should be clearly distinguishable from other displayed information, including those listed in appendix 3.

6 SCALE

6.1 ECDIS should provide an indication if:

(1) the information is displayed at a larger scale than that contained in the ENC;

(2) own ship's position is covered by an ENC at a larger scale than that provided by the display; or

(3) information at own ship's position is not displayed because of applying scale minimum for display.

7 DISPLAY OF OTHER NAVIGATIONAL INFORMATION

7.1 Radar information and/or AIS information may be transferred from systems compliant with the relevant standards of the Organization. Other navigational information may be added to the ECDIS display. However, it should not degrade the displayed system database information and it should be clearly distinguishable from the system database information.

7.2 It should be possible to remove the radar information, AIS information and other navigational information by single operator action.

7.3 ECDIS and added navigational information should use a common reference system. If this is not the case, an indication should be provided.

7.4 Radar

7.4.1 Transferred radar information may contain a radar image and/or tracked target information.

7.4.2 If the radar image is added to the ECDIS display, the chart and the radar image should match in scale, projection and orientation.

7.4.3 The radar image and the position from the position sensor should both be adjusted automatically for antenna offset from the conning position.

8 DISPLAY MODE AND GENERATION OF THE NEIGHBOURING AREA

8.1 It should always be possible to display the system database information in a "north-up" orientation. Other orientations are permitted. When such orientations are displayed, the orientation should be altered in steps large enough to avoid unstable display of the chart information.

8.2 ECDIS should provide for true-motion mode. Other modes are permitted.

8.3 When true-motion mode is in use, reset and generation of the chart display of the neighbouring area should take place automatically at own ship's distance from the edge of the display as determined by the mariner.

8.4 It should be possible to manually change the displayed chart area and the position of own ship relative to the edge of the display.

8.5 If the area covered by the ECDIS display includes waters for which no ENC at a scale appropriate for navigation is available, the areas representing those waters should carry an indication (see appendix 5) to the mariner to refer to the paper chart or to the RCDS mode of operation (see appendix 7).

9 COLOURS AND SYMBOLS

9.1 IHO-recommended colours and symbols should be used to represent system database information. ①

9.2 The colours and symbols other than those mentioned in 9.1 should comply with the applicable requirements contained in the IMO standards for navigational symbols. ②

9.3 ECDIS should allow the mariner to select whether own ship is displayed in true scale or as a symbol.

10 DISPLAY REQUIREMENTS

10.1 ECDIS should be capable of displaying information for:

(1) route planning and supplementary navigation tasks; and

(2) route monitoring.

10.2 The effective size of the chart presentation for route monitoring should be at least 270 mm × 270 mm.

---

① IHO Publication S-52—Specifications for Chart Content and Display Aspects of ECDIS and S-101—Portrayal Catalogue (see appendix 1) and S-98.

② SN. 1/Circ. 243/Rev. 2 on *Guidelines for the presentation of navigational-related symbols, terms and abbreviations*.

10.3 The display should be capable of meeting the colour and resolution recommendations of IHO.[①]

10.4 The method of presentation should ensure that the displayed information is clearly visible to more than one observer in the conditions of light normally experienced on the bridge of the ship by day and by night.

10.5 If information categories included in the standard display (see appendix 2) are removed to customize the display, this should be permanently indicated. Identification of categories which are removed from the standard display should be shown on demand.

11 ROUTE PLANNING, EXCHANGE, MONITORING AND VOYAGE RECORDING

11.1 It should be possible to carry out route planning, route monitoring and exchanging of route plans in a simple and reliable manner.

11.2 The largest scale data available in the system database for the area given should always be used by the ECDIS for all alerts or indications of crossing the ship's safety contour and of entering a prohibited area, and for alerts and indications according to appendix 5.

11.3 Route planning and exchange

11.3.1 It should be possible to carry out route planning including both straight, curved segments and schedule.

11.3.2 It should be possible to adjust a planned route alphanumerically and graphically including:

(1) adding waypoints to a route;

(2) deleting waypoints from a route; and

(3) changing the position of a waypoint.

11.3.3 It should be possible to plan one or more alternative routes in addition to the selected route. The selected route should be clearly distinguishable from the other routes.

11.3.4 It should be possible to exchange, send and receive both selected and alternative route plans with shore-based Maritime Service providers. The exchange

---

① IHO Publication S-52—Specifications for Chart Content and Display Aspects of ECDIS and S-101—Portrayal Catalogue (see appendix 1) and S-98.

ANNEX PERFORMANCE STANDARDS FOR ELECTRONIC CHART DISPLAY AND INFORMATION SYSTEMS (ECDIS)

should be in accordance with standard formats for route plan exchange[①] and should use standard service interfaces including information security protection[②] to allow for secure machine-machine communication. Received route plans should be considered as a basic indication of preferred intention and should be indicated by ECDIS as for voyage planning purposes only. The use of the received route plans should be controlled by the master, in accordance with SOLAS regulations V/34 and V/34-1, respecting the master's professional judgement and discretion.

11.3.5 The exchanged route plan should include a route schedule including estimated time of departure and estimated time of arrival as soon as they can be determined with reasonable accuracy.

11.3.6 A graphical indication is required if the mariner plans a route closer than a user-specified distance from own ship's safety contour.

11.3.7 A graphical indication should be given if the mariner plans a route closer than a user-specified distance from the boundary of a user-selectable category of prohibited area or geographic area for which special conditions exist (see appendix 4). A graphical indication should also be given if the mariner plans a route closer than a user-specified distance from a user-selectable category of point objects, such as a fixed or floating aid to navigation or isolated danger. The user-selectable categories should be the same as the user selections for the display of objects and be based on IHO standards. There should be a permanent indication when any user-selectable categories are deselected. Details of the deselection should be available on demand.

11.3.8 It should be possible for the mariner to select that the indications of 11.3.6 and 11.3.7 take into account accuracy information of relevant hydrographic information, as defined by IHO standards.

11.3.9 It should also be possible to perform a complete route check to support the appraisal and planning process according to the applicable parts of resolution A.893(21). Detected objects should be available for review in graphical form and, on demand, in textual form.

11.3.10 It should be possible for the mariner to specify a cross track limit of deviation from the planned route at which an automatic off-track alarm should be activated.

11.4 Route monitoring

---

① IEC 61174/IEC 63173-1.

② IEC 63173-2.

11.4.1 For route monitoring the selected route and own ship's position should appear whenever the display covers that area.

11.4.2 It should be possible to display a sea area that does not have the ship on the display (e.g. for look ahead, route planning), while route monitoring. If this is done on the display used for route monitoring, the automatic route monitoring functions (e.g. updating ship's position, and providing alerts and indications) should be continuous. It should be possible to return to the route monitoring display covering own ship's position immediately by single operator action.

11.4.3 It should be possible to select that ECDIS gives an alarm and related graphical indication if, within a specified time or distance set by the mariner, own ship will pass closer than a user-selected distance from the safety contour. There should be a permanent indication when the safety contour alarm is deselected.

11.4.4 ECDIS should give a warning or caution, or indication, as selected by the mariner, and related graphical indication if, within a specified time or distance set by the mariner, own ship will pass closer than a user-selected distance from the boundary of a user-selectable category of prohibited area or of a geographical area for which special conditions exist (see appendix 4). The user-selectable categories should be the same as user selections for the display of objects and be based on IHO standards. There should be a permanent indication when any user-selectable categories are deselected. Details of the deselection should be available on demand.

11.4.5 An alarm should be given when the specified cross track limit for deviation from the selected route, if defined by the mariner when route planning, is exceeded.

11.4.6 ECDIS should give a warning or caution or indication as selected by the mariner and related graphical indication if, continuing on its present course and speed, over a specified time or distance set by the mariner, own ship will pass closer than a user-specified distance from a user-selectable category of danger (e.g. obstruction, wreck, rock) that is shallower than the mariner's safety contour or a user-selectable category of aid to navigation. The user-selectable categories should be the same as user selections for the display of objects and be based on IHO standards. There should be a permanent indication when any of the user-selectable categories are deselected. Details of the deselection should be available on demand.

11.4.7 A graphical indication should be given if the current or the next leg of the selected route passes closer than a user-specified distance from the safety contour.

ANNEX PERFORMANCE STANDARDS FOR ELECTRONIC CHART DISPLAY AND INFORMATION SYSTEMS (ECDIS)

11.4.8 A graphical indication should be given if the current or the next leg of the selected route goes closer than a user-specified distance from the boundary of a user-selectable category of prohibited area or a geographic area for which special conditions exist (see appendix 4). A graphical indication should also be given if the selected route goes closer than a user-specified distance from a user-selectable category of point objects, such as a fixed or floating aid to navigation or isolated danger. The user-selectable categories should be the same as user selections for the display of objects and be based on IHO standards.

11.4.9 It should be possible for the mariner to select that the indications of 11.4.3, 11.4.4, 11.4.6, 11.4.7 and 11.4.8 take into account accuracy information of relevant hydrographic information, as defined by IHO standards.

11.4.10 The ship's position should be derived from a continuous positioning system of an accuracy consistent with the requirements of safe navigation. Whenever possible, a second independent positioning source, preferably of a different type, should be provided. In such cases, ECDIS should be capable of identifying discrepancies between the two sources.

11.4.11 ECDIS should provide a warning when the input from position, heading or speed sources is lost. ECDIS should also repeat, but only as an indication, any alerts or indication passed to it from position, heading or speed sources.

11.4.12 A warning should be given by ECDIS when the ship reaches a specified time or distance, set by the mariner, in advance of a critical point on the planned route.

11.4.13 The positioning system and the system database should be on the same geodetic datum. ECDIS should give a warning if this is not the case.

11.4.14 It should be possible to display alternative routes in addition to the selected route. The selected route should be clearly distinguishable from the other routes. During the voyage, it should be possible for the mariner to modify the selected route or change to an alternative route.

11.4.15 If the selected route is changed during the voyage, it should be possible to send the updated route plan to shore-based Maritime Service providers. A route plan received from shore-based Maritime Service providers should only be selected for monitoring after confirmation by the master.

11.4.16 It should be possible to display:

(1) time labels along a ship's track manually on demand and automatically at intervals selected between 1 and 120 minutes; and

(2) an adequate number of points, free movable electronic bearing lines, variable and fixed range markers and other symbols required for navigation purposes and specified in appendix 3.

11.4.17 It should be possible to enter the geographical coordinates of any position and then display that position on demand. Also, it should be possible to select any point (features, symbol or position) on the display and read its geographical coordinates on demand.

11.4.18 It should be possible to adjust the displayed geographic position of the ship manually. This manual adjustment should be indicated alphanumerically on the screen, maintained until altered by the mariner and automatically recorded.

11.4.19 ECDIS should provide the capability to enter and plot manually obtained bearing and distance lines of position (LOP), and calculate the resulting position of own ship. It should be possible to use the resulting position as an origin for dead reckoning.

11.4.20 ECDIS should indicate discrepancies between the positions obtained by continuous positioning systems and positions obtained by manual observations.

11.5 Voyage recording

11.5.1 ECDIS should store and be able to reproduce certain minimum elements required to reconstruct the navigation and verify the official database used during the previous 12 hours. The following data should be recorded at one-minute intervals:

(1) to ensure a record of own ship's past track: time, position, heading, and speed;

(2) to ensure a record of official data used: ENC source, edition, date, cell and update history; and

(3) any changes in safety contour, look ahead and route monitoring alert settings.

11.5.2 ECDIS should output the information listed in 11.5.1 (2) and (3) to a voyage data recorder.

11.5.3 In addition, ECDIS should record the complete track for the entire voyage, with time marks at intervals not exceeding 4 hours.

11.5.4 It should not be possible to manipulate or change the recorded information.

11.5.5 ECDIS should have a capability to preserve the record of the previous 12 hours and the voyage track.

ANNEX PERFORMANCE STANDARDS FOR ELECTRONIC CHART
DISPLAY AND INFORMATION SYSTEMS (ECDIS)

12 CALCULATIONS AND ACCURACY

12.1 The accuracy of all calculations performed by ECDIS should be independent of the characteristics of the output device and should be consistent with the system database accuracy.

12.2 Bearings and distances drawn on the display or those measured between features already drawn on the display should have accuracy no less than that afforded by the resolution of the display.

12.3 The system should be capable of performing and presenting the results of at least the following calculations:

(1) true distance and azimuth between two geographical positions;

(2) geographic position from known position and distance/azimuth; and

(3) geodetic calculations such as spheroidal distance, rhumb line and great circle.

13 PERFORMANCE TESTS, MALFUNCTIONS ALERTS AND INDICATIONS

13.1 ECDIS should be provided with means for either automatically or manually carrying out onboard tests of major functions. In case of a failure, the test should display information to indicate which module is at fault.

13.2 ECDIS should provide a suitable warning or indication of system malfunction.

14 BACKUP ARRANGEMENTS

Adequate backup arrangements should be provided to ensure safe navigation in case of an ECDIS failure; see appendix 6.

(1) Facilities enabling a safe takeover of the ECDIS functions should be provided in order to ensure that an ECDIS failure does not develop into a critical situation.

(2) A backup arrangement should provide means of safe navigation for the remaining part of a voyage in the case of an ECDIS failure.

MODULE C—INTERFACING AND INTEGRATION

15 CONNECTIONS WITH OTHER EQUIPMENT[①]

15.1 ECDIS should not degrade the performance of any equipment providing sensor inputs. Nor should the connection of optional equipment degrade the performance of ECDIS below this standard.

15.2 ECDIS should be connected to the ship's position-fixing system, to the gyro-compass and the speed and distance measuring device. For ships not fitted with a gyro-compass, ECDIS should be connected to a marine transmitting heading device.

15.3 ECDIS may provide a means to supply system database information to external equipment.

16 POWER SUPPLY

16.1 It should be possible to operate ECDIS and all equipment necessary for its normal functioning when supplied by an emergency source of electrical power in accordance with the appropriate requirements of SOLAS chapter II-1.

16.2 Changing from one source of power supply to another or any interruption of the supply for a period of up to 45 seconds should not require the equipment to be manually re-initialized.

[①] Publication IEC 61162.

APPENDIX 1

REFERENCE DOCUMENTS

The following international organizations have developed technical standards and specifications, as listed below, for use in conjunction with this standard. The latest edition of these documents should be obtained from the organization concerned:

INTERNATIONAL MARITIME ORGANIZATION (IMO)

Address: International Maritime Organization
4 Albert Embankment
London SE1 7SR
United Kingdom

Phone: +44 207 735 76 11
Fax: +44 207 587 32 10
Email: info@imo.org
Web: http://www.imo.org

Publications

Resolution MSC. 191 (79), as amended by resolution MSC. 466 (101), on *Performance standards for the presentation of navigation-related information on shipborne navigational displays*

Resolution A. 694 (17) on *Recommendations on general requirements for shipborne radio equipment forming part of the Global Maritime Distress and Safety System (GMDSS) and for electronic navigational aids*

Resolution MSC. 302 (87) on *Performance standards for bridge alert management*

MSC. 1/Circ. 1503/Rev. 2 on *ECDIS—Guidance for good practice*

SN. 1/Circ. 243/Rev. 2 on *Guidelines for the presentation of navigation-related symbols, terms and abbreviations*

MSC/Circ. 982 on *Guidelines on ergonomic criteria for bridge equipment and layout*

INTERNATIONAL HYDROGRAPHIC ORGANIZATION (IHO)

Address: Directing Committee

Phone: +377 93 10 81 00

International Hydrographic Organization
BP 445
MC 98011 Monaco Cedex
Principality of Monaco

Fax：+377 93 10 81 40
Email：info@iho.int
Web：http://www.iho.int

Publications

IHO Publication S-52, Specifications for Chart Content and Display Aspects of ECDIS

IHO Publication S-52 appendix 1, Guidance on Updating the Electronic Navigational Chart

IHO Publication S-52 appendix 2, Colour and Symbol Specifications for ECDIS
IHO Publication S-32, Hydrographic Dictionary
IHO Publication S-57, IHO Transfer Standard for Digital Hydrographic Data
IHO Publication S-100, IHO Universal Hydrographic Data Model
IHO Publication S-101, ENC Product Specification
IHO Publication S-98, Data Product Interoperability in S-100 Navigation Systems
IHO Publication S-61, IHO Product specification for Raster Navigational Charts (RNC)
IHO Publication S-63, IHO Data Protection Scheme
IHO Publication M-3, Resolutions of the IHO
https://iho.int/en/standards-in-force

INTERNATIONAL ELECTROTECHNICAL COMMISSION (IEC)

Address：IEC Central Office
3 rue de Varembe
PO Box 131
CH-1211 Geneva 20
Switzerland

Phone：+41 22 919 02 11
Email：info@iec.ch
Web：www.iec.ch

Publications

IEC Publication 61174, Electronic Chart Display and Information Systems

APPENDIX 1 REFERENCE DOCUMENTS

(ECDIS)—Operational and Performance Requirements, Method of Testing and Required Test Results.

IEC Publication 60945, General Requirements for Shipborne Radio Equipment Forming Part of the Global Maritime Distress and Safety System and Marine Navigational Equipment.

IEC Publication 61162, Digital Interfaces—Navigation and Radiocommunication Equipment Onboard Ship.

IEC Publication 62288, Maritime Navigation and Radiocommunication Equipment and Systems – Presentation of navigation-related information – General requirements, methods of test and required test results.

IEC Publication 63173-1, Maritime Navigation and Radiocommunication Equipment and Systems – Data Interface – Part 1: S-421 Route Plan Based on S-100

IEC Publication 63173-2, Maritime Navigation and Radiocommunication Equipment and Systems – Data Interface – Part 2: Secure Communication Between Ship and Shore

APPENDIX 2

SYSTEM DATABASE INFORMATION AVAILABLE FOR DISPLAY DURING ROUTE PLANNING AND ROUTE MONITORING

1 Display base to be permanently shown on the ECDIS display, consisting of:

(1) coastline (high water);

(2) own ship's safety contour;

(3) isolated underwater dangers of depths less than the safety contour which lie within the safe waters defined by the safety contour;

(4) isolated dangers which lie within the safe water defined by the safety contour, such as fixed structures, overhead wires, etc.;

(5) scale, range and north arrow;

(6) units of depth and height; and

(7) display mode.

2 Standard display consisting of:

(1) display base;

(2) drying line;

(3) buoys, beacons, other aids to navigation and fixed structures;

(4) boundaries of fairways, channels, etc.;

(5) visual and radar conspicuous features;

(6) prohibited and restricted areas;

(7) chart scale boundaries;

(8) indication of cautionary notes;

(9) ships' routeing systems and ferry routes; and

(10) archipelagic sea lanes.

3 All other information, to be displayed individually on demand, for example:

(1) spot soundings;

(2) submarine cables and pipelines;

(3) details of all isolated dangers;

(4) details of aids to navigation;

(5) contents of cautionary notes;

APPENDIX 2 SYSTEM DATABASE INFORMATION AVAILABLE FOR DISPLAY DURING ROUTE PLANNING AND ROUTE MONITORING

(6) ENC edition date;
(7) most recent chart update number;
(8) magnetic variation;
(9) graticule; and
(10) place names.

APPENDIX 3

NAVIGATIONAL ELEMENTS AND PARAMETERS

1 Own ship:
(1) Past track with time marks for primary track.
(2) Past track with time marks for secondary track.
2 Vector for course and speed made good.
3 Variable range marker and/or electronic bearing line.
4 Cursor.
5 Event:
(1) Dead reckoning position and time (DR).
(2) Estimated position and time (EP).
6 Fix and time.
7 Position line and time.
8 Transferred position line and time.
9 Tidal data:
(1) Predicted tidal stream or current vector with effective time and strength.
(2) Calculated tidal stream or current vector with effective time and strength.
10 Danger highlight.
11 Clearing line.
12 Planned course and speed to make good.
13 Waypoint.
14 Distance to run.
15 Planned position with date and time.
16 Position and time of "wheel over".

APPENDIX 4

AREAS FOR WHICH SPECIAL CONDITIONS EXIST

The following are the areas which ECDIS should detect and provide an alert or indication under sections 11.3.7 and 11.4.4:

Traffic separation zone

Inshore traffic zone

Restricted area

Caution area

Offshore production area

Areas to be avoided

User-defined areas to be avoided

Military practice area

Seaplane landing area

Submarine transit lane

Anchorage area

Marine farm/aquaculture

Particularly sensitive sea area (PSSA)

APPENDIX 5

ALERTS AND INDICATORS

Table 1 DEFINITIONS OF ALERTS AND INDICATORS

Section	Requirement	Information
11.4.3	Alarm	Pass closer than set distance from the safety contour
11.4.4	Warning or caution, or indication	Pass closer than set distance from an area with special conditions
11.4.5	Alarm	Deviation from route
11.4.6	Warning or caution, or Indication	Pass closer than set distance from a danger in route monitoring mode
11.4.11	Warning	Positioning system failure
11.4.12	Warning	Approach to critical point
11.4.13	Warning	Different geodetic datum
13.2	Warning or indication	Malfunction of ECDIS
5.8 (3)	Indication	Default safety contour
6.1 (1)	Indication	Information overscale
6.1 (2)	Indication	Larger scale ENC available
6.1 (3)	Indication	Information not displayed owing to scale minimum
7.3	Indication	Different reference system
8.5	Indication	No ENC available
10.5	Indication	Customized display
11.3 6	Indication	Route planning closer than set distance from the safety contour
11.3.7	Indication	Route planning closer than set distance from specified area
11.4.7	Indication	Monitored route pass closer than set distance from the safety contour

APPENDIX 5 ALERTS AND INDICATORS

续上表

Section	Requirement	Information
11.4.8	Indication	Monitored route pass closer than set distance from a specified area or danger
13.1	Indication	System test failure

In this Performance Standard, the definitions of Indicators and Alerts provided in resolution A. 1021 (26) *Code on Alerts and Indicators*, 2009 and resolution MSC. 302(87) *Performance standards for bridge alert management* apply.

Alert: Audible and/or visual announcement of a condition requiring attention. Priorities of alert are alarm, warning and caution.

Indication: Visual indication giving information about the condition of a system or equipment.

APPENDIX 6

BACKUP REQUIREMENTS

1 INTRODUCTION

As prescribed in section 14 of this performance standard, adequate independent backup arrangements should be provided to ensure safe navigation in case of ECDIS failure. Such arrangements include:

(1) facilities enabling a safe takeover of the ECDIS functions in order to ensure that an ECDIS failure does not result in a critical situation; and

(2) a means to provide for safe navigation for the remaining part of the voyage in case of ECDIS failure.

2 PURPOSE

The purpose of an ECDIS backup system is to ensure that safe navigation is not compromised in the event of ECDIS failure. This should include a timely transfer to the backup system during critical navigation situations. The backup system should allow ships to be navigated safely until the termination of the voyage.

3 FUNCTIONAL REQUIREMENTS

3.1 Required functions and their availability

3.1.1 Presentation of chart information

The backup system should display in graphical (chart) form the relevant information of the hydrographic and geographic environment which are necessary for safe navigation.

3.1.2 Route planning

The backup system should be capable of performing the route planning functions, including:

(1) taking over of the route plan originally performed on the ECDIS; and

(2) adjusting a planned route manually or by transfer from a route planning

APPENDIX 6 BACKUP REQUIREMENTS

device.

3.1.3 Route monitoring

The backup system should enable a takeover of the route monitoring originally performed by the ECDIS, and provide at least the following functions:

(1) plotting own ship's position automatically, or manually on a chart;

(2) taking courses, distances and bearings from the chart;

(3) displaying the planned route;

(4) displaying time labels along ship's track; and

(5) plotting an adequate number of points, bearing lines, range markers, etc., on the chart.

3.1.4 Display information

If the backup is an electronic device, it should be capable of displaying at least the information equivalent to the standard display as defined in this performance standard.

3.1.5 Provision of chart information

(1) The chart information to be used in the backup arrangement should be the latest edition, as corrected by official updates, of that issued by or on the authority of a government, authorized hydrographic office or other relevant government institution, and conform to IHO standards.

(2) It should not be possible to alter the contents of the electronic chart information.

(3) The chart or chart data edition and issuing date should be indicated.

3.1.6 Updating

The information displayed by the ECDIS backup arrangements should be up to date for the entire voyage.

3.1.7 Scale

If an electronic device is used, it should provide an indication:

(1) if the information is displayed at a larger scale than that contained in the database; and

(2) if own ship's position is covered by a chart at a larger scale than that provided by the system.

3.1.8 If radar and other navigational information are added to an electronic backup display, all the corresponding requirements for radar information and other navigation information of this performance standard should be met.

3.1.9 If an electronic device is used, the display mode and generation of the neighbouring area should be in accordance with section 8 of this performance standard.

3.1.10　Voyage recording

The backup arrangements should be able to keep a record of the ship's actual track, including positions and corresponding times.

3.2　Reliability and accuracy

3.2.1　Reliability

The backup arrangements should provide reliable operation under prevailing environmental and normal operating conditions.

3.2.2　Accuracy

Accuracy should be in accordance with section 12 of this performance standard.

3.3　Malfunctions, alerts and indications

If an electronic device is used, it should provide a suitable warning or indication of system malfunction.

4　OPERATIONAL REQUIREMENTS

4.1　Ergonomics

If an electronic device is used, it should be designed in accordance with the ergonomic principles of ECDIS.

4.2　Presentation of information

If an electronic device is used:

(1) colours and symbols should be in accordance with the colours and symbols requirements of ECDIS; and

(2) the effective size of the chart presentation should be not less than 270 mm × 270 mm or 270 mm diameter.

5　POWER SUPPLY

If an electronic device is used:

(1) the backup power supply should be separate from the ECDIS; and

(2) it should conform to the requirements in this ECDIS performance standard.

6 CONNECTIONS WITH OTHER EQUIPMENT

6.1 If an electronic device is used, it should:

(1) be connected to the ship's position-fixing system, to the gyro-compass and to the speed and distance measuring device. For ships not fitted with a gyro-compass, ECDIS should be connected to a marine transmitting heading device; and

(2) not degrade the performance of any equipment providing sensor input.

6.2 If radar with selected parts of the ENC chart information overlay is used as an element of the backup, the radar should comply with resolution MSC. 192(79).

APPENDIX 7

RCDS MODE OF OPERATION

Whenever in this appendix reference is made to any provisions of the annex related to ECDIS, the term ECDIS should be substituted by the term RCDS, system database by SRNC and ENC by RNC, as appropriate.

This appendix refers to each paragraph of the performance standards for ECDIS (i. e. the annex to which this part is appendix 7) and specifies which paragraphs of the annex either:

(1) apply to RCDS; or
(2) do not apply to RCDS; or
(3) are modified or replaced as shown in order to apply to RCDS.

Any additional requirements applicable to RCDS are also described.

1 SCOPE

1.1 Paragraph applies to RCDS.

1.2 When operating in RCDS mode, an appropriate portfolio of up-to-date paper charts (APC) should be carried on board and be readily available to the mariner.

1.3 – 1.6 Paragraphs apply to RCDS.

1.7 RCDS should provide appropriate alerts or indications with respect to the information displayed or malfunction of the equipment (see table 1 of this appendix).

1.8 Refers to appendix 7 and applies to RCDS.

2 APPLICATION OF THESE STANDARDS

2.1 – 2.4 Paragraphs apply to RCDS.

3 DEFINITIONS

3.1 Raster chart display system (RCDS) means a navigation information system displaying RNCs with positional information from navigation sensors to assist

APPENDIX 7 RCDS MODE OF OPERATION

the mariner in route planning and route monitoring, and if required, display additional navigation-related information.

3.2 Raster navigational chart (RNC) means a facsimile of a paper chart originated by, or distributed on the authority of, a government-authorized hydrographic office. RNC is used in these standards to mean either a single chart or a collection of charts.

3.3 Paragraph does not apply to RCDS.

3.4 System raster navigational chart database (SRNC) means a database resulting from the transformation of the RNC by the RCDS to include updates to the RNC by appropriate means.

3.5 – 3.6 Paragraphs do not apply to RCDS.

3.7 Paragraph applies to RCDS.

3.8 Appropriate portfolio of up-to-date paper charts (APC) means a suite of paper charts of a scale to show sufficient detail of topography, depths, navigational hazards, aids to navigation, charted routes and routeing measures to provide the mariner with information on the overall navigational environment. The APC should provide adequate look ahead capability. Coastal States will provide details of the charts which meet the requirement of this portfolio, and these details are included in a worldwide database maintained by the IHO. Consideration should be given to the details contained in this database when determining the content of the APC.

MODULE A—DATABASE

4 PROVISION AND UPDATING OF CHART INFORMATION

4.1 The RNC used in RCDS should be the latest edition of that originated by, or distributed on the authority of, a government-authorized hydrographic office and conform to IHO standards. RNCs not on WGS 84 or PE-90 should carry metadata (i.e. additional data) to allow georeferenced positional data to be displayed in the correct relationship to SRNC data.

4.2 The contents of the SRNC should be adequate and up to date for that part of the intended voyage not covered by ENC.

4.3 It should not be possible to alter the contents of the RNC.

4.4 – 4.7 All paragraphs apply to RCDS.

4.8 Paragraph does not apply to RCDS.

MODULE B—OPERATIONAL AND FUNCTIONAL REQUIREMENTS

5　DISPLAY OF SRNC INFORMATION

5.1　RCDS should be capable of displaying all SRNC information.

5.2　SRNC information available for display during route planning and route monitoring should be subdivided into two categories:

(1) the RCDS standard display consisting of RNC and its updates, including its scale, the scale at which it is displayed, its horizontal datum, and its units of depths and heights; and

(2) any other information such as mariner's notes.

5.3 – 5.4　Paragraphs apply to RCDS.

5.5　It should be easy to add to, or remove from, the RCDS display any information additional to the RNC data, such as mariner's notes. It should not be possible to remove any information from the RNC.

5.6 – 5.10　Paragraphs do not apply to RCDS.

5.11　Paragraph applies to RCDS.

5.12　RCDS should provide a means to ensure that the RNC and all updates to it have been correctly loaded into the system RNC.

5.13　The RNC and all updates to it should be clearly distinguishable from other displayed information, including those listed in appendix 3.

5.14　There should always be an indication if the ECDIS equipment is operating in RCDS mode.

6　SCALE

This section applies to RCDS.

7　DISPLAY OF OTHER NAVIGATIONAL INFORMATION

7.1 – 7.4　All paragraphs apply to RCDS.

8 DISPLAY MODE AND GENERATION OF THE NEIGHBOURING AREA

8.1 It should always be possible to display the SRNC in "chart-up" orientation. Other orientations are permitted.

8.2 – 8.4 All paragraphs apply to RCDS.

8.5 Paragraph refers to RCDS mode of operation.

9 COLOURS AND SYMBOLS

9.1 IHO-recommended colours and symbols should be used to represent SRNC information.

9.2 Paragraph applies to RCDS.

9.3 Paragraph applies to RCDS.

10 DISPLAY REQUIREMENTS

10.1 – 10.2 Paragraphs apply to RCDS.

10.3 Paragraph does not apply to RCDS.

10.4 Paragraph applies to RCDS.

10.5 Paragraph does not apply to RCDS.

10.6 RCDS should be capable of displaying, simply and quickly, chart notes which are not located on the portion of the chart currently being displayed.

11 ROUTE PLANNING, EXCHANGE, MONITORING AND VOYAGE RECORDING

11.1 Paragraphs apply to RCDS.

11.2 Paragraph does not apply to RCDS.

11.3 Route planning

11.3.1 – 11.3.5 Paragraphs apply to RCDS.

11.3.6 – 11.3.9 Paragraphs do not apply to RCDS.

11.3.10 Paragraph applies to RCDS.

11.4 Route monitoring

11.4.1 Paragraph applies to RCDS.

11.4.2 It should be possible to display a sea area that does not have the ship on the display (e.g. for look ahead, route planning), while route monitoring. If this is done on the display used for route monitoring, the automatic route monitoring functions in 11.4.11 and 11.4.12 should be continuous. It should be possible to return to the route monitoring display covering own ship's position immediately by single operator action.

11.4.3 – 11.4.4 Paragraphs do not apply to RCDS.

11.4.5 Paragraph applies to RCDS.

11.4.6 – 11.4.9 Paragraphs do not apply to RCDS.

11.4.10 – 11.4.12 Paragraphs apply to RCDS.

11.4.13 The RCDS should only accept positional data referenced to the WGS 84 or PE-90 geodetic datum. RCDS should give a warning if the positional data is not referenced to one of these datum. If the displayed RNC cannot be referenced to the WGS 84 or PE-90 datum then a continuous indication should be provided.

11.4.14 – 11.4.18 Paragraphs apply to RCDS.

11.4.19 RCDS should allow the user to manually align the SRNC with positional data. This can be necessary, for example, to compensate for local charting errors.

11.4.20 It should be possible to activate an automatic warning when the ship crosses a point or line, or is within the boundary of a mariner entered feature within a specified time or distance.

11.5 Voyage recording

11.5.1 – 11.5.4 All paragraphs apply to RCDS.

12 CALCULATIONS AND ACCURACY

12.1 – 12.3 All paragraphs apply to RCDS.

12.4 RCDS should be capable of performing transformations between a local datum and WGS 84 datum.

13 PERFORMANCE TESTS, MALFUNCTION ALARMS AND INDICATIONS

13.1 – 13.2 All paragraphs apply to RCDS.

APPENDIX 7   RCDS MODE OF OPERATION

14   BACKUP ARRANGEMENTS

All paragraphs apply to RCDS.

MODULE C—INTERFACING AND INTEGRATION

15   CONNECTIONS WITH OTHER EQUIPMENT

15.1 – 15.3   All paragraphs apply to RCDS.

16   POWER SUPPLY

16.1 – 16.2   All paragraphs apply to RCDS

Table 1   ALERTS AND INDICATORS IN THE RCDS MODE OF OPERATION

Section	Requirement	Information
11.4.5	Alarm	Deviation from route
11.4.20	Warning	Approach to mariner entered feature, e.g. area, line
11.4.11	Warning	Position system failure
11.4.12	Warning	Approach to critical point
11.4.13	Warning or indication	Different geodetic datum
13.2	Warning or indication	Malfunction of RCDS mode
5.13	Indication	ECDIS operating in the raster mode
6.1	Indication	Larger scale information available, or overscale
6.1 (2)	Indication	Larger scale RNC available for the area of the ship

Note: The definitions of alerts and indicators are given in appendix 5.

ECDIS 良好实践指南

海上安全委员会通函草案
ECDIS 良好实践指南

1 海上安全委员会在其第 95 届会议（2015 年 6 月 3 日至 12 日）上，将之前的 7 份 ECDIS 通函中的相关指南汇总成一份独立的综合性文件，并批准为《ECDIS 良好实践指南》。

2 电子海图显示与信息系统（ECDIS）是一个复杂的、与安全相关的、基于软件的系统，具有多种显示和集成选项。持续安全、有效地使用 ECDIS 涉及多方主体，包括海员、设备厂商、海图制作机构、软硬件维护供应商、船主和运营商，以及培训机构。相关方均需明确其在 ECDIS 方面的作用和责任。

3 2002 年，ECDIS 被认为可满足《国际海上人命安全公约》（以下简称《SOLAS 公约》）第 V/19 条的海图配备要求。多年来，IMO 成员国、海道测量机构、设备厂商和其他组织持续推动制定各种与 ECDIS 相关的指南，IMO 还发布了一系列关于 ECDIS 的补充通函。

4 与 ECDIS 相关的 IMO 指南大多数是以渐进的方式制定的，这些信息应尽可能被整合，以便在一份通函中提供较为综合的 ECDIS 相关指南。综合性指南的形式，一方面有利于指南信息更新，避免信息重复以及交叉参考等问题；另一方面，这种信息整合方式有助于使用者更加清晰地理解 ECDIS 的配备要求和使用规则。

5 《ECDIS 良好实践指南》是本通函的附件之一。鼓励广大海员使用本指南，以提高对 ECDIS 的理解和安全操作水平。

6 海上安全委员会第 98 届会议（2017 年 6 月 7 日至 16 日），根据人的因素、培训和值班分委会（Sub-Committee on Human Element, Training and Watchkeeping）第 4 次会议（2017 年 1 月 30 日至 2 月 3 日）提出的建议、经修订的 1978 年《STCW 公约》中对于 ECDIS 熟悉度的要求，以及《ISM 规则》，批准了《ECDIS 良好实践指南》第 1 次修订版，该修订版以 MSC.1/Circ.1503/Rev.1 的名称发布。

7 海上安全委员会第 106 届会议（2022 年 11 月 2 日至 11 日），根据航行、通信和搜救分委会（Sub-Committee on Navigation, Communications and Search and Rescue）第 9 次会议（2022 年 6 月 21 日至 30 日）提出的建议，为明确船载 ECDIS 更新的一般原则、程序和文件来证明其持续符合规定等因素，批准了《ECDIS 良好实践指南》第 2 次修订版，如附件所述。

8 请 IMO 组织成员（以下简称本组织成员）和《SOLAS 公约》所有缔约国政府提醒所有相关组织注意本通函。特别请港口国向港口监察员提供该指南，并请船旗国向船主、船长、官方承认的组织以及船旗国控制检查员和测量员提供该指南。本通函电子版下载地址为：https://docs.imo.org/Category.aspx?cid=106。

9 本通函取代 MSC.1/Circ.1503/Rev.1。

附 件

ECDIS 良好实践指南

（第 2 次修订版）

引 言

1 通过提交至本组织的正式安全评估和多年来自愿使用 ECDIS 积累的经验，认识到使用 ECDIS 导航有不可否认的安全效益。早在 2008 年 7 月 1 日，高速船（HSC）已要求配备 ECDIS。随后，从 2012 年 7 月 1 日起，HSC 以外的船舶，开始分阶段强制要求配备 ECDIS（根据《SOLAS 公约》第 V/19.2.10 条，配备要求取决于船舶类型、大小和建造日期）。

2 ECDIS 是一个复杂的、与安全相关的、基于软件的系统，具有多种显示和集成功能。持续安全、有效地使用 ECDIS 涉及多方主体，包括海员、设备厂商、海图制作机构、软硬件维护供应商、船主和运营商，以及培训机构。重要的是，要让所有这些利益相关方对他们在 ECDIS 方面的作用和责任有明确和共同的理解。

3 《ECDIS 良好实践指南》（以下简称"指南"）将之前的 7 份 ECDIS 通函中的相关指南汇总成为一份独立的综合性文件。该指南分为 8 个部分，即：

    A 《SOLAS 公约》关于海图配备的要求
    B ECDIS 软件的维护
    C 船载 ECDIS 更新
    D ECDIS 的异常操作识别
    E RCDS 和 ECDIS 之间的差异
    F ECDIS 培训
    G 从纸质海图到 ECDIS 导航的转换
    H 关于实际使用 ECDIS 模拟器的培训和评估的指导意见

4 本指南旨在帮助船舶顺利安装 ECDIS 并实现安全、有效的使用。建议配备 ECDIS 的船舶的操作员、船长和甲板人员参考本指南，以提高对 ECDIS 的理解并确保安全、有效使用。

5 虽然本指南取代了 7 份与 ECDIS 相关的 IMO 通函，但仍有其他 IMO 的通函在不同程度上涉及 ECDIS 事项，必要时也应参考这些通函。参考部分提供了一份清单，列出了 ECDIS 性能标准和与 ECDIS 相关的其他 IMO 通函。

A 《SOLAS 公约》关于海图配备的要求

6 根据《SOLAS 公约》第 V/19.2.10 条的要求，ECDIS 的强制配备将在 2012 年 7 月 1 日至 2018 年 7 月 1 日期间分阶段生效。根据《SOLAS 公约》第 V/18 条和 V/19 条，船舶若使用 ECDIS 来满足海图配备的要求，该 ECDIS 设备必须符合 IMO 的相关性能标准。根据安装日期，船载 ECDIS 必须符合经修订的 A.817（19）号决议、MSC.232（82）号或 MSC.530（106）/Rev.1 号决议的要求。从本质上讲，船载 ECDIS 要满足《SOLAS 公约》的海图配备要求，它必须：

（1）获得型号认可；
（2）使用最新版电子海图（ENC）；
（3）定期保养以符合国际海道测量组织（IHO）最新标准；和
（4）有完善、独立的备用系统。

7 根据《SOLAS 公约》第 V/18 条，船载 ECDIS 必须经过型号认证。型号认证是船载 ECDIS 符合 IMO 性能标准的前提认证程序。该认证程序由船旗国认可的型号认证组织或船级社根据国际电工委员会（IEC）等制定的相关测试标准（例如 IEC 61174）执行。

8 根据《SOLAS 公约》第 V/19.2.1.4 条规定，船舶必须配备规划航程所需的所有海图。根据《SOLAS 公约》第 V/2.2 条，海图是由政府、授权海道测量机构或其他有关政府机构正式发布的航海出版物。需要或者选择使用 ECDIS 的船舶应配备电子海图，如果电子海图不可用或者其比例尺不适合制定和显示航行计划，则应配备栅格海图（RNC）和/或必要的纸质海图。

9 IHO 提供在线海图目录，详细说明了海图的覆盖范围，并提及沿海国关于纸质海图要求的指导意见（如有）。该目录还提供了 IHO 成员国网站的链接用于获取更多信息。IHO 在线海图目录的访问链接为：https://iho.int/en/iho-online-catalogues。

10 根据《SOLAS 公约》第 V/27 条规定，规划航程所需的海图应是充分且最新的。对于使用 ECDIS 的船舶，所有 ENC 和 RNC 必须是最新版本，并使用电子海图更新（例如 ENC 更新），航海通告也要保持更新。此外，ECDIS 软件应保持最新状态，以能够根据 IHO 的海图内容和显示标准，正确显示更新的电子海图。

11 ECDIS 性能标准的相关附录具体规定了独立备用系统的要求，以确保

ECDIS 故障时的航行安全。要求包括：（1）能够安全接管 ECDIS 功能的设施，避免 ECDIS 故障引发危急情况；（2）当 ECDIS 发生故障时，保障剩余航程安全完成。上文第 10 条提到的更新要求也适用于备用系统配置。

B ECDIS 软件的维护

12 运行中的 ECDIS 包括硬件、软件和数据。在安全导航方面，重要的是保证 ECDIS 中的应用软件完全按照性能标准工作，并且能够显示 ENC 中包含的所有相关数字信息。

13 未更新到最新版本 IHO 标准的 ECDIS 可能不符合《SOLAS 公约》第 V/19.2.1.4 条规定的海图配备要求。

14 例如，2007 年 1 月发布的 IHO ENC 产品规范附件 1，采用了在 ENC 内列入 IMO 最近提出的对特别敏感海域和群岛航道的要求，以适应未来航行安全的任何要求。

15 ECDIS 未更新至符合最新版本的 IHO ENC 产品规范或兼容的显示库，可能会导致其无法正确显示最新的海图要素。此外，即使已更新 ENC，也可能无法激活相应的警报和提示。同样，未更新至符合最新版本的 IHO 数据保护标准的 ECDIS，可能无法解密或正确验证某些电子海图，从而导致无法加载或安装。可从 IHO 网站访问与 ECDIS 相关的最新 IHO 标准清单：www.iho.int (https://iho.int/en/standards-in-force)。

16 安全导航要求制造商提供可确保软件维护充分的机制。制造商可以通过建立网站提供软件版本信息，这些信息应包括已经执行的 IHO 标准。

17 为确保 ECDIS 符合性能标准进行的所有更新，制造商应特别标识并传达给指定的系统用户。

18 主管部门应告知船主和运营商，ECDIS 软件维护是一项重要事务，船长、船主和运营商应根据《国际安全管理（ISM）规则》（以下简称《ISM 规则》）采取适当措施。

C 船载 ECDIS 更新

19 在更新船载 ECDIS 模块之前，无论是需要与现行的 IHO 标准兼容还是由制造商发起的以改进功能或修复小错误的更新，制造商都应通报型号认可证书（TAC）上指定的型号认可机构（TAA），并提供相关信息和技术文档。由 TAA 评估并决定是否需进行额外测试。

20 根据 TAA 的评估和判断：

(1) 如果需要进行额外测试，
    TAA 应签发以下文件之一：
    ①新的 TAC，其中包含更新的软件和/或硬件详细信息；或
    ②一封包含更新软件和/或它的硬件细节的批准函（LOA），以补充原 TAC；
(2) 如果不需要进行额外测试，也不需要新的 TAC 或 LOA，TAA 应通过电子邮件或其他方式，以书面形式通知制造商。

21 在上述第 20（1）条的情况下，制造商应发出新的符合性声明（DOC），声明相关产品符合国际指南的要求。如第 20（2）条所述，当 TAA 没有发出新的 TAC 或 LOA 时，制造商应保留 TAA 书面通知的副本。附录 4 中列出了船载 ECDIS 更新的示例。

22 为了证明船载的 ECDIS 更新是一致的，应提供以下信息之一：
(1) 新的 TAC，其中包含更新的软件和硬件详细信息，以及新的 DOC；
(2) 旧的 TAC，以及对其进行补充的 LOA 和新的 DOC；或
(3) 旧的 TAC 和 DOC。

23 制造商应向船舶提供上述文件的副本和更新的用户手册，直到设备从船上移走，并提供 TAA 就第 20（2）条所述的更改做出的书面决定（如有要求）。此外，制造商还应按照第 16 条的要求通过网站提供此类信息。

24 建议制造商通过二维码、电子邮件或现场工程师向船舶提供第 22 条所列文件的副本。每个 ECDIS 模块的二维码可便捷地查询每台设备的硬件/软件更新信息。

D ECDIS 异常运行的识别

25 目前，已经发现了一些 ECDIS 异常运行的情况。由于 ECDIS 的复杂性，特别是它涉及硬件、软件和数据的组合，可能存在其他异常情况。

26 这些异常情况在按照 ECDIS 性能标准［经修订的 A.817（19）号决议，即 2009 年之前］建造和经型号认证的 ECDIS 设备中尤为明显。同时，经修订的 ECDIS 性能标准［MSC.232（82）号和 MSC.530（106）/Rev.1 号决议］仍然容易受到附录 1 中规定的限制。

27 ECDIS 异常是由 ECDIS 设备的意外情况或用户的无意行为造成的，这可能会影响设备的使用或用户的导航决策。包括但不限于以下情况：
(1) 无法正确显示导航功能，例如：
    ①IMO 最新认定的导航区域，如 PSSA 和 ASL；
    ②具有复杂特性的航行灯标；和

③水下要素和孤立危险物；

（2）在航程规划模式下"航线检查"功能未能识别障碍物；

（3）未能正确发出警报；和

（4）无法正确管理多个警报。

28 这种异常现象的存在表明，必须维护 ECDIS 软件，以确保该软件能够按照 IHO 最新的海图内容和显示标准正确显示电子海图。建议设备制造商进行适当的检查，这对于仅配备 ECDIS 作为唯一可用海图信息来源的船舶尤其重要。

29 如果 ECDIS 软件或硬件的故障对海上安全、健康或环境构成风险，那么制造商应尽早通知船旗国主管部门、管理机构和 ECDIS 用户，并协商制定适当的缓解措施。

30 由于 ECDIS 配备要求的广泛应用和实施，委员会认为，必须向有关当局报告海员发现的异常情况，并由有关当局进行调查，以确保该情况得到解决。制造商应建立相应机制，以确保向已识别的 ECDIS 用户通报异常情况，并进行相关升级。船长、船主和运营商应依据制造商提供的软件维护指南来检查此类升级是否可用。

31 为了更好地了解问题的严重程度，请主管部门收集、调查和发布有关 ECDIS 异常的信息。主管部门或管理机构应：

（1）建议船旗国的船舶报告 ECDIS 异常情况，并提供 ECDIS 设备和 ENC 的详细信息，以便进行分析；

（2）对报告者的身份予以保密；

（3）如有需要，同意与其他 IMO 成员国和国际组织共享信息；和

（4）当 ECDIS 出现异常、可能影响航行安全时，向海员发出警报。

E RCDS 和 ECDIS 的差异

32 ECDIS 可以在以下两种模式下运行：

（1）使用 ENC 时的 ECDIS 模式；和

（2）当 ENC 不可用而改用 RNC 时的 RCDS 模式。

尽管近年来 ENC 的覆盖范围迅速扩大，但某些区域可能仍未发布详细的 ENC。

33 RCDS 模式不具备 ECDIS 的全部功能，只能与最新纸质海图结合使用。RCDS 模式的局限性详见附录2。

F ECDIS 培训

34 以下信息旨在协助成员国、经修订的 1978 年《STCW 公约》缔约方、航运公司和海员确保其向配备 ECDIS 的船舶上的船长和甲板管理人员①提供的关于使用 ECDIS 的培训计划满足经修订的 1978 年《STCW 公约》强制性培训要求：

（1）根据《STCW 公约》规定，所有负责 500 总吨或以上船舶航行值班的高级船员必须具备使用海图和航海出版物的全面知识和能力（参见《STCW 公约》，表 A-Ⅱ/1）；

（2）负责航行值班的船长和高级船员（包括管理和操作级别）至少应接受 ECDIS 通用培训，以满足《STCW 公约》2010 年马尼拉修正案的能力要求；

（3）《STCW 公约》2010 年马尼拉修正案加强了 ECDIS 培训要求，并为管理和操作级别的高级船员新增了多项使用 ECDIS 的额外能力要求（参见《STCW 公约》，表 A-Ⅱ/1 和 A-Ⅱ/2）。该修正案培训要求自 2013 年 7 月 1 日起生效；

（4）根据《STCW 公约》第二章要求，获得证书的船长和高级船员应熟悉包括 ECDIS 在内的船舶设备（《STCW 公约》第Ⅰ/64 条）；

（5）《STCW 公约》第Ⅰ/14 条第 1.5 款以及《国际安全管理（ISM）规则》第 6.3 节要求公司确保海员熟悉船载 ECDIS 设备，包括其备用装置、传感器和相关外围设备。建议 ECDIS 制造商提供培训资源，包括特定类型的材料，并将这些资源作为 ECDIS 培训的一部分；

（6）《STCW 公约》第Ⅰ/14 条第 1.4 款要求公司保留培训佐证资料，并确保该资料随时可查询。对于有效期超过 2017 年 1 月 1 日的能力证书，港口国监管局应将该证书视为海员能力达标的初步佐证资料；

（7）公司还应按照《STCW 公约》第Ⅰ/14 条第 1.5 款的要求，保留海员对 ECDIS 熟悉情况的培训佐证资料；

（8）有关当局应告知港口国管制人员上文第 6 条详述的 ECDIS 培训要求；和

（9）提请注意：

STCW.7/Circ.16 号通函——阐明与《STCW 公约》2010 年马尼拉修正案有关的过渡性规定；

---

① 未配备 ECDIS 的船舶上的人员不需要参加 ECDIS 培训和评估。该限制体现在发给相关海员的签注中（参见 STCW 规则的表 A-Ⅱ/1 和 A-Ⅱ/2）。

STCW.7/Circ.17 号通函——就过渡安排向港口国管制官员提供咨询意见，以便于 2017 年 1 月 1 日全面执行《STCW 公约》2010 年马尼拉修正案的要求；和

STCW.7/Circ.24/Rev.1 号通函——为缔约方、主管部门、港口国管制当局、相关组织和其他有关各方提供的关于经修订的 1978 年《STCW 公约》要求的指南。

G 从纸质海图到 ECDIS 导航的过渡

35 首先，船主和运营商应该对从纸质海图转变为 ECDIS 导航所涉及的问题进行评估。船长和甲板管理人员应参加相关评估，以反映 ECDIS 实际使用人的关注点或需求。这个过程将有助于尽早了解要解决的问题，并帮助船长和甲板管理人员为转变导航方式做好准备。

36 记录对问题的评估并制定标准的 ECDIS 作业流程，将有助于建立完善的 ECDIS 导航规范，简化对船长和甲板管理人员的培训，并促进工作顺利交接。

37 此外，船主和运营商应向船长和甲板管理人员提供 ECDIS 通用培训和 ECDIS 熟悉培训计划，以便船长和甲板管理人员能充分了解如何使用 ECDIS 进行航线规划和导航。

38 除了国内和国际规则和条例、IMO 关于 ECDIS 操作使用的示范课程 1.27 和 IMO 性能标准外，IHO 还发布了一份在线出版物《关于电子海图和配备要求的示例》。它是关于 ECDIS 硬件、培训和电子海图数据技术方面的推荐信息来源。可从各种渠道免费下载该在线出版物，包括：https://iho.int/en/standards-and-specifications。

39 船主和运营商应始终关注所在国家主管部门关于 ECDIS 配备和使用的最新信息。

F ECDIS 模拟器的操作培训和评估指南

40 当使用模拟器进行 ECDIS 操作培训或评估时，应遵循以下暂行指南。

41 在实际使用 ECDIS 模拟器开展培训和评估时：

（1）ECDIS 模拟设备的使用；和

（2）符合不低于下文第 42 条和第 43 条规定的标准。

42 ECDIS 模拟设备除了满足经修订的《STCW 公约》第 A-I/12 节规定的所有适用性能标准外，还应能够模拟满足本组织适用性能标准的导航设备和

驾驶台操作控制装置，并具备水深测定功能，以及：

（1）建立实时操作环境，包括适用于航行任务的导航系统、通信指引和设备，以及待执行的值班任务和需评估的操作能力；和

（2）能够真实地模拟开放水域条件下的本船特性，以及天气、潮汐流和洋流的影响。

43　应适当地使用模拟器进行 ECDIS 的演示和实践。培训活动最好实时进行，以提高参训人员对不当使用 ECDIS 的危害的认识。另外，加速模式只能用于演示环节。

44　详细指南见附录 3。

附录 1

ECDIS 显示操作和显示异常清单

（不按优先级排序）

本清单中，第 1、2、3、4、5（b）、6、7 和 11 条已与 2011 年 11 月 IHO DPPC 数据集进行了核对：

1　无法正确显示 ASL 或 PSSA 等 IMO 批准的功能符号——未安装最新版 IHO 演示库的 ECDIS 设备将无法显示正确的符号，而会显示问号（?）或无任何显示。在某些情况下，ECDIS 可能无法加载包含此类数据的 ENC。但设备型号认证不受演示库版本的影响。

解决方法——使用"选择报告"功能或参考纸质海图/出版物查询"?"。

2　某些 ECDIS 设备对于险恶地和障碍物的显示不正确——某些 ECDIS 型号在标准显示模式下无法按预期显示水下要素（但仍会触发相应警报）。这些要素仅在使用"全部"或"其他"显示模式时显示。在某些情况下，会使用不同的符号来表示这些特征。

解决方法——使用"全部"或"其他"显示模式。

3　在某些情况下，一些搁浅/危险的残骸和障碍物可能无法在任何模式下显示；这种情况仅限于来自单个制造商的某些 ECDIS 版本，该制造商已发布软件补丁解决该问题。

解决方法——使用纸质海图。

4　在某些 ECDIS 设备中，位于等深线上的物体可能无法在"标准"模式下显示。

解决方法——使用"全部"或"其他"显示模式。

附录1 ECDIS 显示操作和显示异常清单（不按优先级排序）

5 小型（点状）陆地区域，尤其是那些仅以小比例尺（使用范围1和2）描绘的区域，ENC 可能无法清晰显示，并且在某些 ECDIS 设备中，在航线规划或航线监控模式下可能无法触发警报：

（a）小型陆地特征可能会被其他海图细节（例如要素名称或等高线标注）遮挡；和

（b）一些 ECDIS 设备可能不会对小型 ENC 执行航线检查，因此可能不会发出警告，导致陆地区域可能无法在航线监控期间被"前视"功能识别。

解决方法——手动仔细检查可用的最大比例ENC。

出于上述第5（a）条提到的 ECDIS 的限制，海员（即使是使用最新系统的）应使用"其他/全部"显示模式对整个航线计划仔细进行目视检查，以确保该航线计划和在偏离航线计划时没有危险。

6 光扇区的彩色弧线显示不正确——某些 ECDIS 可能无法显示复杂灯光的彩色弧线。这在跨越0/360度（北向）的地方尤其普遍。

解决方法——使用"选择报告"功能检查光扇区。

7 一些早期版本的 ECDIS 模型无法正确显示以 ENC 编码的时间变量数据。例如，可能无法正确显示开始和结束日期，这些要素被用于在 ENC 中进行新增航线安排，导致旧实例和新实例同时显示。IEC61174 版本1中未包含此项测试。

解决方法——使用"选择报告"功能确定起止日期/时间。

8 部分早期版本的 ECDIS 仅支持逗号分隔的潮流数据样式，难以解读和使用。

解决方法——使用ECDIS 外置的潮流图谱。

9 海员可能不容易看到锚地、泊位和航道名称的显示，并且可能无法显示最大旋回圈半径。

解决方法——使用"全部"或"其他"显示模式和"选择报告"功能获取旋回圈信息；通过VTS/ 港务局的通信确认必要名称。

10 与短距扇区灯相比，360 度陆标灯的对比度不足。

解决方法——海员要注意使用"选择报告"来验证灯光特性。

11 ENC 可能包括某些浅滩探测，特别是报告的深度，这些探测的编码方式使其不会在"标准"模式下显示，即使深度小于安全等深线设置，也可能无法触发警报。大多数海道测量部门已向 IHO 报告更新相关 ENC，以确保在标准模式下可以显示重要的深度。

解决方法——在显示所有探测的显示模式下运行ECDIS。

12 在某些 ECDIS 中，没有已知深度值的险恶地可能会被描述为孤立危险物，并在"标准"模式下显示，这可能会导致不必要的界面混乱。

解决方法——没有针对混乱界面的解决方法，海员要注意并使用"选择报告"功能来确定该要素是否存在危险。

13 不同制造商的 ECDIS 在显示浅滩水域孤立危险物时，符号系统可能存在差异。

解决方法——海员在这些区域作业时要保持警惕，并使用"全部"或"其他"显示模式。

14 当在加载了较大比例尺覆盖范围的 ECDIS 中打开了较小比例尺的 ENC 时，可能会出现界面混乱问题。当用户缩小比例时，界面混乱问题会更加明显。这是因为各个制造商的 ENC 加载策略和各个 ENC 制作者的编码策略存在差异。如果水文机构在海图要素上使用 SCAMIN（最小比例）属性，那么这个问题将得到最小化。IHO 标准规定 ECDIS 不应打开编译比例与使用中的显示比例尺显著不同的 ENC 数据。在未来这可以通过采用基于 ENC 内定义的比例范围的标准化 ENC 加载策略来进行改进。

解决方法——在航线监控期间使用标准显示模式并适度（但不要过度）使用缩放功能来改善这种情况。该技术已包含在关于ECDIS操作使用的IMO1.27号示范课程教学大纲中。

15 在某些 ECDIS 设备中，电子海图中某些注释的文本可能会被截断或完全不显示，使海员无法知悉。

解决方法——暂无可行的解决方法；海员发现此问题时，应告知ENC服务商。

16 不必要的警报和提示——海员的反馈表明，ECDIS 会发出非必要和干扰性警报。这是由于同时应用了 ECDIS 性能标准和 ENC 编码要求。在根据修订后的性能标准［MSC.232（82）号决议］设计的 ECDIS 中，海员可以对警报和提示的数量进行一些设置，但该功能常被忽视。

解决方法——IMO1.27 号示范课程介绍了在ECDIS 操作中最大程度减少警报的方法。

附录 2

栅格海图显示系统（RCDS）和 ECDIS 的区别

海员需注意 RCDS 模式的以下限制：

1 与没有显示边界的 ENC 不同，RNC 基于纸质海图，因此在 ECDIS 中会有明显的边界；

2 RNC 不会自动触发警报（如防搁浅警报）。然而，在航线规划中可以手动设置发出警报和提示，例如避险线、船舶安全等深线、孤立危险物标记和危险区域，从而应对这些限制；

3 RNC 之间的水平基准与海图投影可能不同。海员应该了解海图的水平基准如何与使用中的定位系统的基准相关联。在某些情况下，这可能涉及位置显示的变化。此外，这种不同在网格交点处最为明显；

4 由于许多 RNC 不能参考 WGS-84 或 PE 90 大地基准面，因此 ECDIS 需要持续提示；

5 不能通过移除要素来简化 RNC 显示以适应特定的导航环境或当前的任务，因为这会影响雷达/ARPA 的叠加；

6 同一比例的海图固定不变时，本船前视功能可能会受限制，不便于海员确定距离和方位或辨别远处物体；

7 RCDS 显示方向不是海图向上时，会影响海图文本和符号的可读性（例如航向向上、航线向上）；

8 无法通过查询 RNC 特征以获取有关海图对象的其他信息。因此，在规划航线过程中（无论是使用 ENC 还是 RNC），海员都应查阅所有相关出版物（例如航行指南等）；

9 除非在航线规划时海员手动输入船舶安全等深线或者安全深度，否则在使用 RNC 时，无法直接在显示屏上显示和突出这些特征；

10 不同来源的 RNC 会使用不同的颜色来显示相似的海图信息。海图信息在白天和夜间使用的颜色也可能不同；

11 RNC 应按照对应纸质海图的原来比例使用。过度放大或缩小海图会严重降低显示图像的质量。如果 RNC 以比纸质海图更大的比例显示，则 ECDIS 会发出提示；

12 ECDIS 在 ENC 中发出提示时，海员应确定海道测量数据的可信度。在使用 RNC 时，海员应查阅源数据图或置信区间图等（如有）。

附录 3

ECDIS 模拟器的操作培训和评估指南

概述

ECDIS 培训项目的目标

1　ECDIS 参训人员应能够：

（1）操作 ECDIS 设备，使用 ECDIS 的导航功能，选择和评估所有相关信息，并在发生故障时采取适当措施；

（2）陈述显示数据的潜在错误和常见的表述错误；和

（3）解释为什么不应将 ECDIS 作为唯一可靠的导航辅助工具。

理论与实践

2　为了安全使用 ECDIS，相关人员需要了解和理解管理 ECDIS 数据的基本原理及其表示规则，以及显示数据中的潜在错误、与 ECDIS 相关的限制和潜在危险，因此，应开展一些涵盖理论解释的培训讲座。这类课程应尽可能在参训人员熟悉的场景下开展，并讲解实际案例。此外，应在模拟器演练中加强参训人员对这些理论知识的应用。

3　为了安全操作 ECDIS 设备和处理 ECDIS 相关信息（使用 ECDIS 的导航功能、选择和评估所有相关信息、熟悉 ECDIS 的人机交互等），应将 ECDIS 模拟器的实践练习和培训作为课程的主要内容。

4　为了明确培训目标，应确定课程的结构。课程的每个主题都应该有详细的学习目标。

模拟器练习

5　应在单个 ECDIS 模拟器或包含 ECDIS 的全任务导航模拟器上进行练习，让参训人员获得必要的实践技能。对于实时导航练习，建议使用全任务导航模拟器，以涵盖各种复杂的导航情况。应在各种比例尺、导航模式和显示模式下进行全面练习，使参训人员能够在各种情况下使用设备。

6 练习场景的选择取决于手头上可用的模拟器。如果有各类 ECDIS 设备和全任务模拟器，ECDIS 设备应主要用于 ECDIS 的基本练习和航线计划，而全任务模拟器可用于与实时航线监控相关的练习。在整个培训计划中，练习的复杂程度应逐渐增加，直到参训人员全面掌握学习目标的所有相关内容。

7 参训人员在练习时应尽可能有真实的感受。为了实现这一目标，练习场景可以是虚构的海域。可将各类海域发生的各类情况、涉及的功能和实际操作整合到一个场景中，提供实时练习体验，以达到不同学习目标。

8 模拟器练习的主要目的是确保参训人员了解其在操作使用 ECDIS 时的安全责任，并熟悉其使用的系统和设备。

ECDIS 的主要类型和显示特性

9 参训人员应了解 ECDIS 的主要类型，以及其显示特性、数据结构，并熟悉以下内容：

（1）矢量图和栅格图之间的差异；
（2）ECDIS 和 ECS 之间的差异；
（3）ECDIS 和 RCDS 之间的差异；
（4）不同类型 ECDIS 的特性；和
（5）特殊用途系统的特性（异常情况/紧急情况）。

过度依赖 ECDIS 的风险

10 ECDIS 操作培训应注意：
（1）ECDIS 作为导航工具的局限性；
（2）系统异常运行的潜在风险；
（3）系统的局限性，包括传感器的局限性；
（4）海道测量数据不准确；矢量图和栅格电子海图的局限性（ECDIS 与 RCDS、ENC 与 RNC）；和
（5）人为失误的风险。
应强调保持正确瞭望和定期检查（特别是船舶的位置）的必要性。

检测虚假信息

11 了解 ECDIS 设备的局限性和检测虚假信息对于安全使用 ECDIS 至关

重要。培训时应强调以下方面：

（1）ECDIS 设备的性能标准；

（2）电子海图上的雷达数据表示，并消除雷达图像与电子海图之间的差异；

（3）电子海图和纸质海图之间可能存在的投影差异；

（4）显示电子海图及其原始比例时可能出现的比例差异（比例过大和比例过小）；

（5）使用不同定位参考系统的效果差异；

（6）使用不同水平和垂直基准面的效果差异；

（7）船舶在海上航行的影响；

（8）栅格图显示模式下 ECDIS 的限制；

（9）显示下列信息时的潜在错误：

　①本船位置；

　②雷达数据、ARPA 和 AIS 信息；

　③不同大地坐标系；和

（10）验证手动或自动数据校正的结果：

　①海图数据与雷达图的对比；和

　②使用其他独立的定位系统检查本船的位置。

12 分析数据的错误推断以及为避免错误推断应采取的适当行动。应强调以下情况可能的后果：

（1）忽略显示画面比例过度放大；

（2）不加判断地接受本船位置；

（3）显示模式混乱；

（4）海图比例尺混乱；

（5）参考系混乱；

（6）不同的呈现方式；

（7）不同的矢量模式；

（8）真北和电罗经北（雷达）之间的差异；

（9）使用相同的数据参考系统；

（10）使用适当的海图比例尺；

（11）根据给定的情况和条件使用最合适的传感器；

（12）输入正确的安全数值：

　①本船的安全等深线；

　②安全深度（安全水域）；和

　③事件记录；和

(13）正确使用所有可用数据。

13　应认识到 RCDS 仅为导航辅助工具。在 RCDS 模式下运行时，应将 ECDIS 设备与最新纸质海图一起使用：

（1）了解附录 2 中描述的 RCDS 模式的操作差异；和

（2）在任何模式下的 ECDIS 都应该与最新海图结合使用。

系统性能和精度的影响因素

14　应基本了解 ECDIS 的基本原理，并全面掌握以下实践知识：

（1）启动和设置 ECDIS；连接数据传感器：卫星和无线电导航系统接收器、雷达、电罗经、计程仪、回声测深仪等；这些传感器的精度和局限性，包括测量误差和船舶位置精度的影响、操纵对航向指示器性能精度的影响、罗盘误差对航向指示精度的影响、浅水对计程仪性能精度的影响、计程仪、校正对航速计算精度的影响、海况对回声测深仪性能精度的影响；和

（2）本组织现时采用的 ECDIS 性能标准[①]。

实践

显示设置和维护

15　应具备的知识和技能：

（1）ECDIS 信息界面获得最佳显示效果的正确启动程序；

（2）选择显示呈现方式（标准显示、基础显示、按需显示其他信息）；

（3）正确调整可变雷达/ARPA 的显示控件，以优化数据显示；

（4）便捷配置选择；

（5）选择在 ECDIS 中输入所需的速度；

（6）矢量时间尺度的选择；和

（7）位置、雷达/ARPA、指南针、速度输入传感器和 ECDIS 的性能检查。

电子海图的操作使用

16　应具备的知识和技能：

---

① 参见本组织通过的相关性能标准。

(1) ECDIS 数据显示的主要特征和为导航任务选择合适的信息；
(2) 监测船舶安全所需的自动化功能，例如位置、航向/电罗经航向、速度、安全值和时间的显示；
(3) 手动功能（通过光标、电子方位线、距离圈）；
(4) 电子海图内容的选择和修改；
(5) 调整比例尺（包括缩小比例和放大比例）；
(6) 缩放功能；
(7) 本船安全参数的设置；
(8) 白天或夜间显示模式切换；
(9) 熟悉所有海图符号和缩写；
(10) 使用不同种类的光标和电子选项获取航行数据；
(11) 从不同方向查看区域并返回本船位置；
(12) 通过地理坐标定位指定区域；
(13) 显示航行情况所需的数据；
(14) 选择合适和准确的数据（位置、航向、速度等）；
(15) 输入航海日志；
(16) 使用北向上显示方式和其他方向的显示方式；和
(17) 使用真实运动和相对运动模式。

航线规划

17 应具备的知识和技能：
(1) 将船舶特性加载至 ECDIS；
(2) 选择进行航线规划的海域：
　①查阅海上航线经过的水域；和
　②海图比例尺的转换；
　③验证海图更新；
　④在 ECDIS 显示器上规划航线，使用图形编辑器并考虑恒向线和大圆圈航行：
　　.1 使用 ECDIS 数据库获取导航、水文气象和其他数据；
　　.2 在海图比例尺上显示时，考虑转弯半径和转弯点/线；
　　.3 标记危险深度和区域，并展示防护深度等深线；
　　.4 用交叉深度等深线和关键交叉航迹偏差标记航路点，或通过添加、替换和删除航路点进行标记；
　　.5 考虑安全航速；

.6 检查预先规划的安全航线；和
.7 发出警报和警告；

⑤包含表格形式数据的航线计划，包括：
.1 航路点选择；
.2 回顾航路点列表；
.3 规划说明；
.4 航线规划的调整；
.5 检查预先规划的航行航线；
.6 备选航线规划；
.7 保存规划航线、加载或删除航线；
.8 生成监控界面的图像副本并打印航线；
.9 规划航线的编辑和修改；
.10 根据船舶的尺寸和操纵参数设定安全值；
.11 返航规划；和
.12 连接多条航线。

航线监控

18 应具备的知识和技能：
（1）使用独立数据定位船舶或使用替代 ECDIS 的系统；
（2）使用前视功能：
①切换海图及其比例尺；
②查阅海图；
③矢量时间选择；
④预测船舶在一段时间内的位置；
⑤更改预先计划的航线（航线调整）；
⑥输入独立数据以计算风压差和流压差；
⑦对警报做出正确响应；
⑧对大地基准面的差异进行修正；
⑨在船舶航线上显示时间标记；
⑩手动输入船舶位置；和
⑪在海图上测量坐标、航向、方位和距离。

警报处理

19 应具备解读和正确应对各种警报系统的知识和能力,例如导航传感器、提示器、数据和海图警报,以及提示器警告,包括打开/关闭声音和视觉警报信号系统,具体情况如下:

(1) ECDIS 数据库中缺少下一张海图;
(2) 穿越安全等深线;
(3) 超过偏航限制范围;
(4) 偏离规划航线;
(5) 接近航路点;
(6) 接近临界点;
(7) 到达航路点的计算时间与实际时间之间存在差异;
(8) 比例尺过小或过大的提示信息;
(9) 接近孤立危险物或危险区域;
(10) 穿越特定区域;
(11) 选择不同的大地基准面;
(12) 接近其他船舶;
(13) 值班结束;
(14) 切换计时器;
(15) 系统测试失败;
(16) ECDIS 中使用的定位系统发生故障;
(17) 航位推算失败;和
(18) 无法通过导航系统确定船舶位置。

手动校正船舶位置和移动参数

20 手动校正模式下应具备的知识和技能:
(1) 当卫星和无线电导航系统接收器关闭时,在航位推算模式下的修正船舶位置;
(2) 当自动获取的坐标不准确时的船舶位置修正;和
(3) 航向和速度值修正。

船舶计程仪记录

21 应具备的知识和技能：
(1) 自动航程记录；
(2) 历史航迹重建，包括：
①记录媒介；
②记录间隔；
③验证使用的数据库；
(3) 查看电子船舶计程仪中的记录；
(4) 电子船舶计程仪的即时记录；
(5) 更改船舶时间；
(6) 输入补充数据；
(7) 打印电子船舶计程仪的内容；
(8) 设置自动记录时间间隔；
(9) 航行数据的汇总和报告；和
(10) 与航行数据记录器（VDR）的连接。

海图更新

22 应具备的知识和技能：
(1) 手动更新电子海图。应特别注意海图和校正文本参考椭球体一致性和测量单位统一；
(2) 使用符合电子海图格式的数据，对电子海图进行半自动更新；和
(3) 使用通过电子数据通信线路获得的更新文件，对电子海图进行自动更新。
当使用未更新的数据导致危急情况时，应要求参训人员具备对海图进行临时更新的能力。

雷达/ARPA 连接下的 ECDIS 操作

23 应具备的知识和技能：
(1) 将 ARPA 连接到 ECDIS；
(2) 提示目标的速度矢量显示；
(3) 提示目标的航迹显示；

（4）目标航迹存档；
（5）查看目标列表；
（6）检查雷达覆盖范围与电子海图地理特征的一致性；
（7）模拟一项或多项操作；
（8）使用 ARPA 捕获的参考点修正本船位置；和
（9）使用 ARPA 的光标和电子操作杆进行修正。

另见《STCW 公约》第 B-I/12 节，关于使用模拟器的指南（适用于雷达和 ARPA），尤其是第 17 至第 19 条和第 36 至第 38 条。

连接 AIS 的 ECDIS 操作使用

24 应具备的知识和技能：
（1）连接 AIS；
（2）解释 AIS 数据；
（3）提示目标的速度矢量显示；
（4）提示目标的航迹显示；和
（5）目标航迹存档。

操作警告及其优点和局限性

25 参训人员应了解 ECDIS 操作警告的用途、优点和局限性，并能正确设置（如适用），以避免受误报信息干扰。

系统运行测试

26 应具备的知识和技能：
（1）测试 ECDIS 故障的方法，包括功能自检；
（2）发生故障后应采取的预防措施；和
（3）充分的备用系统使用方案（使用备用系统接管和导航）。

汇报练习

27 教员应分析参训人员完成练习的情况并打印结果报告。讲评时间应该占模拟器练习总时间的 10% 至 15%。

附录4

ECDIS 更新操作示例

以下为 ECDIS 更新和相关记录的示例：

示例1

TAC 列出了软件 5.03.xx 的版本号系列，当前制造商软件版本号为 5.03.02，并将更新至 5.03.03。

制造商报告：制造商报告针对最新 IHO 标准进行的微小错误修复或更改。

TAA 决定：TAA 认为该更新是微小更新，不需要重新认证或获取 LOA。

提供的文件：原 TAC、DOC 软件。

软件版本号从 5.03.02 更改为 5.03.03，仍属原 TAC 规定的 5.03.xx 版本号系列。

示例2

TAC 列出了软件 5.03.xx 的版本号系列，当前制造商软件版本号为 5.03.02，并将更新至 5.04.00。

制造商报告：制造商报告新增功能或对现有功能的更新。

TAA 决定：TAA 认为该更新与 TAC 相关，需要进行额外的测试和重新认证。

提供的文件：新版 TAC 和新版 DOC。

软件版本号从 5.03.02 更改为 5.04.00，新版 TAC 更新的 5.04.xx 系列。

示例3

TAC 列出了 IHO 标准版 3.0.x，当前制造商 IHO 标准版为 3.0.(1) 并且需要更新到 3.1.(0) 版。

制造商报告：制造商报告针对 IHO 最新要求进行的更新。

TAA 决定：TAA 认为该更新是与 TAC 相关的重大更新，需要重新测试。

提供的文件：有 LOA 补充文件的原 TAC，新版 DOC。

IHO 标准版本从 3.0.(1) 更改至 3.1.(0)，记录于 LOA 文件。

示例 4

制造商使用 5.0 版本软件制造了 ECDIS，然后将制造软件更改为 6.0 版本，但是硬件配置保持不变。在本例中，新版 TAC 列表 v6.0.xx 替代 v5.0.xx。

制造商报告：制造商报告软件从 5.0 版本更新到 6.0 版本。

TAA 决定：TAA 认为该更新是与 TAC 相关的重大更新，需要重新认证。

提供的文件：新版 TAC 和新版 DOC。

在新版 TAC 中，软件版本号从 5.0 更改为 6.0。

参考文件

IMO 的 ECDIS 性能标准

1　A.817（19）号决议：电子海图与信息系统（ECDIS）性能标准
2　MSC.64（67）号决议：关于新的和修订的性能标准的建议
3　MSC.86（70）号决议：通过新的和修订的航行设备性能标准
4　MSC.232（82）号决议：通过修订的电子海图与信息系统（ECDIS）性能标准
5　MSC.530（106）/Rev.1 号决议：电子海图与信息系统（ECDIS）性能标准

与 ECDIS 相关的其他 IMO 通函

1　MSC.1/Circ.982：驾驶台设备与布置的人机工程学衡准指南
2　MSC.1/Circ.1091：在船上引入新技术时需要考虑的问题
3　MSC.1/Circ.1221：船用产品型号认可证书的有效性
4　MSC.1/Circ.1389：船载导航和通信设备更新程序指南
5　SN.1/Circ.213：海图基准和海图位置的精度指南
6　SN.1/Circ.243/Rev.1：与航行有关的符号、术语和缩写的显示指南
7　SN.1/Circ.255：关于海图基准和海图位置精度的附加指南
8　SN.1/Circ.265：关于将 SOLAS 规则 V/15 条应用于 INS、IBS 和驾驶台设计的指南
9　SN.1/Circ.288：驾驶台设备和系统及其布置和集成（BES）指南

ANNEX 23

DRAFT MSC CIRCULAR
ECDIS—GUIDANCE FOR GOOD PRACTICE

1　The Maritime Safety Committee, at its 95th session (3 to 12 June 2015), approved the *ECDIS—Guidance for Good Practice*, drawing together relevant guidance from seven previous ECDIS circulars into a single, consolidated document.

2　ECDIS is a complex, safety-relevant, software-based system with multiple options for display and integration. The ongoing safe and effective use of ECDIS involves many stakeholders including seafarers, equipment manufacturers, chart producers, hardware and software maintenance providers, shipowners and operators, and training providers. It is important that all these stakeholders have a clear and common understanding of their roles and responsibilities in relation to ECDIS.

3　In 2002, ECDIS was accepted as meeting the chart carriage requirements of SOLAS regulation V/19. Over the years, IMO Member States, hydrographic offices, equipment manufacturers and other organizations contributed to the development of guidance on a variety of ECDIS-related matters and IMO issued a series of complementary circulars on ECDIS.

4　While most useful IMO guidance on ECDIS was developed in this incremental manner, the information needed to be consolidated, where possible, to have ECDIS-related guidance within a single circular, which could be easily kept up to date without duplication or need for continual cross-referencing. Such consolidation of information offers clear and unambiguous understanding of the carriage requirements and use of ECDIS.

5　The consolidated guidance termed "*ECDIS—Guidance for Good Practice*" is set out in the annex to this circular. Ship operators, masters and deck officers on ECDIS-fitted ships are encouraged to use this guidance to improve their understanding and facilitate safe and effective use of ECDIS.

6　The Maritime Safety Committee, at its 98th session (7 to 16 June 2017), based on a recommendation made by the Sub-Committee on Human Element, Training and Watchkeeping, at its 4th session (30 January to 3 February 2017), and noting the need to clarify the requirement of ECDIS familiarization as specified in the STCW Convention, 1978, as amended, and the ISM Code, approved the revision 1 of the *ECDIS—Guidance for Good Practice*, which was disseminated as MSC. 1/Circ. 1503/Rev. 1.

7 The Maritime Safety Committee, at its 106th session (2 to 11 November 2022), based on a recommendation made by the Sub-Committee on Navigation, Communications and Search and Rescue, at its 9th session (21 to 30 June 2022), and noting the need to clarify the general principle, procedures and documentation for onboard ECDIS updates to demonstrate ongoing compliance, approved the revision 2 of the *ECDIS—Guidance for Good Practice*, as set out in the annex.

8 Members of the Organization and all Contracting Governments to the SOLAS Convention are invited to bring this circular to the attention of all entities concerned. In particular, port States are invited to make the guidance available to their port State control inspectors, and flag States to shipowners, masters, recognized organizations, flag State control inspectors and surveyors. An electronic copy of this circular can be downloaded from the Organization's document website at: https://docs.imo.org/Category.aspx?cid=106.

9 This circular supersedes MSC. 1/Circ. 1503/Rev. 1.

ANNEX

ECDIS—GUIDANCE FOR GOOD PRACTICE

(REVISION 2)

INTRODUCTION

1 The undeniable safety benefits of navigating with electronic chart display and information systems (ECDIS) were recognized through Formal Safety Assessments submitted to the Organization and experience gained by the voluntary use of ECDIS for many years. ECDIS was mandated for carriage by high-speed craft (HSC) as early as 1 July 2008. Subsequently, the mandatory carriage of ECDIS for ships other than HSC (depending on the ship type, size and construction date, as required by SOLAS regulation V/19.2.10) commenced in a phased manner from 1 July 2012 onwards.

2 ECDIS is a complex, safety-relevant, software-based system with multiple options for display and integration. The ongoing safe and effective use of ECDIS involves many stakeholders including seafarers, equipment manufacturers, chart producers, hardware and software maintenance providers, shipowners and operators, and training providers. It is important that all these stakeholders have a clear and common understanding of their roles and responsibilities in relation to ECDIS.

3 This *ECDIS—Guidance for Good Practice*, referred to as "Guidance" hereafter, draws together relevant guidance from seven previous ECDIS circulars into a single, consolidated document. The guidance is laid out in eight sections, namely:

    A   Chart carriage requirement of SOLAS
    B   Maintenance of ECDIS software
    C   Onboard ECDIS updates
    D   Operating anomalies identified within ECDIS
    E   Differences between raster chart display system (RCDS) and ECDIS
    F   ECDIS training
    G   Transitioning from paper chart to ECDIS navigation

H   Guidance on training and assessment in the operational use of ECDIS simulators

4   This guidance is intended to assist the smooth implementation of ECDIS and its ongoing safe and effective use on board ships. Ship operators, masters and deck officers on ECDIS-fitted ships are encouraged to use this guidance to improve their understanding and facilitate the safe and effective use of ECDIS.

5   Although this guidance replaces seven IMO ECDIS-related circulars, there remain several other IMO circulars that also address ECDIS matters to varying degrees, and reference should also be made to these circulars where necessary. A list containing the IMO ECDIS performance standards and the other IMO circulars that relate to ECDIS is provided in the reference section.

A   CHART CARRIAGE REQUIREMENT OF SOLAS

6   The mandatory carriage of ECDIS, as required by SOLAS regulation V/19.2.10, is subject to a staged entry into force between 1 July 2012 and 1 July 2018. As per SOLAS regulations V/18 and V/19, for a ship to use ECDIS to meet the chart carriage requirements of SOLAS, the ECDIS equipment must conform to the relevant IMO performance standards. Depending on the date of their installation, ECDIS units on board are required to comply with performance standards set out in resolutions A.817(19), as amended, MSC.232(82) or MSC.530 (106)/Rev.1. Essentially, where an ECDIS is being used to meet the chart carriage requirements of SOLAS, it must:

(1) be type-approved;

(2) use up-to-date electronic nautical charts (ENCs);

(3) be maintained so as to be compatible with the latest applicable International Hydrographic Organization (IHO) standards; and

(4) have adequate, independent backup arrangements in place.

7   According to SOLAS regulation V/18, ECDIS units on board ships must be type-approved. Type approval is the certification process that ECDIS equipment must undergo before it can be considered as complying with IMO performance standards. The process is carried out by flag Administration-accredited type approval organizations or marine classification societies in accordance with the relevant test standards developed by, inter alia, the International Electrotechnical Commission (IEC) (e.g. IEC 61174).

8   In accordance with SOLAS regulation V/19.2.1.4, ships must carry all

nautical charts necessary for the intended voyage. As defined by SOLAS regulation V/2.2, nautical charts are issued officially by or on the authority of a government, authorized hydrographic office or other relevant government institutions. Ships required to fit ECDIS and ships choosing to use ECDIS to meet the chart carriage requirements of SOLAS should carry ENCs or, where ENCs are not available at all or are not of an appropriate scale for the planning and display of the ship's voyage plan, raster navigational charts (RNC) and/or any needed paper charts should be carried.

9 IHO provides an online chart catalogue that details the coverage of ENCs together with references to coastal State guidance on any requirements for paper charts (where this has been provided). The catalogue also provides links to IHO Member States' websites where additional information may be found. The IHO online chart catalogue can be accessed from the IHO website at: https://iho.int/en/iho-online-catalogues.

10 As per SOLAS regulation V/27, all nautical charts necessary for the intended voyage shall be adequate and up to date. For ships using ECDIS to meet the chart carriage requirement of SOLAS, all ENCs and RNCs must be of the latest available edition and be kept up to date using both the electronic chart updates (e.g. ENC updates) and the latest available notices to mariners. Additionally, ECDIS software should be kept up to date such that it is capable of displaying up-to-date electronic charts correctly according to the latest version of IHO's chart content and display standards.

11 Relevant appendices of IMO performance standards for ECDIS specify the requirements for adequate independent backup arrangements to ensure safe navigation in case of ECDIS failure. Such arrangements include: (1) facilities enabling a safe takeover of the ECDIS functions in order to ensure that an ECDIS failure does not result in a critical situation; (2) a means to provide for safe navigation for the remaining part of the voyage in case of ECDIS failure. The update requirements mentioned in paragraph 10 above applies to the backup arrangements as well.

B MAINTENANCE OF ECDIS SOFTWARE

12 ECDIS in operation comprises hardware, software and data. It is important for the safety of navigation that the application software within ECDIS works fully in accordance with the performance standards and is capable of displaying all the relevant digital information contained within the ENC.

13 ECDIS that is not updated to the latest version of the IHO standards may not meet the chart carriage requirements as set out in SOLAS regulation V/19.2.1.4.

14 For example, in January 2007, Supplement No.1 to the IHO ENC Product Specification was introduced in order to include, within the ENC, the then recently introduced IMO requirements for particularly sensitive sea areas (PSSA) and archipelagic sea lanes (ASL) and to cater for any future safety of navigation requirements.

15 Any ECDIS which is not upgraded to be compatible with the latest version of the IHO ENC Product Specification or the Presentation Library may be unable to correctly display the latest charted features. Additionally, the appropriate alarms and indications may not be activated even though the features have been included in the ENC. Similarly, any ECDIS which is not updated to be fully compliant with the latest version of the IHO Data Protection Standard may fail to decrypt or to properly authenticate some ENCs, leading to failure to load or install. An up-to-date list of all the relevant IHO standards relating to ECDIS equipment can be accessed from the IHO website: www.iho.int (https://iho.int/en/standards-in-force.)

16 The need for safe navigation requires that manufacturers should provide a mechanism to ensure that software maintenance arrangements are adequate. This may be achieved through the provision of software version information using a website. Such information should include the IHO standards which have been implemented.

17 Any updates, essential to make an ECDIS compliant with the performance standards, should be particularly identified and be actively communicated to identified users of the system.

18 Administrations should inform shipowners and operators that proper ECDIS software maintenance is an important issue and that adequate measures need to be implemented by masters, shipowners and operators in accordance with the International Safety Management (ISM) Code.

C ONBOARD ECDIS UPDATES

19 Prior to the onboard ECDIS units being updated, whether required to be compatible with the in force IHO standards or initiated by the manufacturer to improve functions or fix minor bugs, the manufacturer should notify the type approval authority (TAA) named on the type approval certificate (TAC) of any modification or changes to the equipment, together with the relevant information and technical

documentation. Accordingly, after assessment, the TAA decides if and what level of additional testing is required in each individual case.

20 Depending on the assessment and judgement of the TAA:

(1) if additional testing is needed and performed and conformity is demonstrated, the TAA should issue one of the following documents:

① a new TAC with the updated software and/or hardware details on it; or

② a Letter of Acceptance (LOA) with the updated software and/or hardware details on it to supplement the old TAC;

(2) if no additional testing is required and no new TAC or LOA is necessary, the TAA should inform the manufacturer of the decision in writing, via email or other means of notification.

21 In cases of paragraph 20 (1) above, the manufacturer should issue a new declaration of conformity (DOC), declaring that the product concerned is in conformity with the requirements of the international instruments that apply to it. When no new TAC or LOA is issued by the TAA as indicated in paragraph 20 (2), the manufacturer should keep a copy of the written notification by the TAA. Examples of onboard ECDIS updates are listed in appendix 4.

22 To prove that an ECDIS update on board is conformant, one of the following should be made available:

(1) a new TAC with the updated software and hardware details on it and new DOC;

(2) the old TAC supplemented by an LOA and new DOC; or

(3) the old TAC and DOC.

23 Manufacturers should provide a copy of the documents above and an updated user manual, if applicable, to the ship to be carried on board until the equipment is removed from the ship and make available the written decision taken by the TAA regarding the minor changes as described in paragraph 20 (2), if so requested. In addition, such information should also be made available by the manufacturer using a website as required by paragraph 16.

24 Manufacturers are also encouraged to provide a copy of the documents listed in paragraph 22 to the ship via a QR code, email or field engineer. A QR code for each ECDIS unit would be particularly useful to provide easier access to information in relation to the hardware/software updates of each equipment.

D OPERATING ANOMALIES IDENTIFIED WITHIN ECDIS

25 A number of ECDIS operating anomalies have been identified. Due to the complex nature of ECDIS, and in particular because it involves a mix of hardware, software and data, it is possible that further anomalies may exist.

26 These anomalies are particularly apparent in ECDIS units that have been built and type-approved to ECDIS Performance Standards [resolution A. 817(19), as amended], (i. e. before 2009). However, ECDIS units type-approved to the revised ECDIS Performance Standards [resolutions MSC. 232(82) and MSC. 530 (106)/Rev. 1] are still vulnerable to the limitations as set out in appendix 1.

27 An ECDIS anomaly is an unexpected or unintended behaviour of an ECDIS unit which may affect the use of the equipment or navigational decisions made by the user. Examples include, but are not limited to:

(1) failure to display a navigational feature correctly, such as:
　①navigation areas recently recognized by IMO such as PSSA and ASL;
　②navigational lights with complex characteristics; and
　③underwater features and isolated dangers;

(2) failure to detect objects by "route checking" in voyage planning mode;

(3) failure to alarm correctly; and

(4) failure to manage a number of alarms correctly.

28 The existence of such anomalies highlights the importance of maintaining ECDIS software to ensure that it is capable of displaying up-to-date electronic charts correctly according to the latest version of the IHO's chart content and display standards. It is recommended that appropriate checks be made with the equipment manufacturer. This is of particular importance where ECDIS is the only source of chart information available.

29 A manufacturer should notify the flag Administration, ROs and identified ECDIS users at the earliest possible opportunity to communicate if the ECDIS presents a risk to maritime safety, to health or to the environment due to a malfunction of software or hardware including appropriate mitigation measures.

30 Given the widespread use and the implementation of the ECDIS carriage requirement, the Committee considered it important that any anomalies identified by mariners are reported to and investigated by the appropriate authorities to ensure their

resolution. Manufacturers should have a mechanism in place to ensure they notify identified users of their ECDIS systems about any noted anomalies and close out subsequently with relevant upgrades. Masters, shipowners and operators should use the software maintenance arrangements provided by the manufacturer to check if such upgrades are available.

31 In order to better understand the extent of the issue, Administrations are invited to collect, investigate and disseminate information about ECDIS anomalies. Administrations or designated bodies are invited to:

(1) encourage vessels under their flag to report such anomalies, with sufficient detail on the ECDIS equipment and ENCs, to allow analysis;

(2) treat the identity of the reporter as confidential;

(3) agree to share information with other IMO Member States and international organizations on request; and

(4) issue alerts to mariners where such anomalies might affect safety of navigation.

E DIFFERENCES BETWEEN RASTER CHART DISPLAY SYSTEM (RCDS) AND ECDIS

32 ECDIS may be operated in one of the two modes:

(1) the ECDIS mode when ENCs are used; and

(2) the RCDS mode when ENCs are not available and RNCs are used instead.

Although in recent years ENC coverage has increased rapidly, there could be some areas for which suitably detailed ENCs may not have been issued.

33 The RCDS mode does not have the full functionality of ECDIS and can only be used together with an appropriate portfolio of up-to-date paper charts. Limitations of the RCDS mode are set out in appendix 2.

F ECDIS TRAINING

34 The information provided below aims to assist Member States, Parties to the 1978 STCW Convention, as amended, companies and seafarers in ensuring that

training programmes on the use of ECDIS provided to masters and deck officers[①] serving on ships fitted with ECDIS meet the mandatory training requirements of the 1978 STCW Convention, as amended:

(1) under the provisions of the STCW Convention and Code, all officers in charge of a navigational watch on ships of 500 gross tonnage or more must have a thorough knowledge and ability to use nautical charts and nautical publications (refer STCW Code, Table A-Ⅱ/1);

(2) masters and officers in charge of a navigational watch (both at management and operational level) serving on ships fitted with ECDIS should as a minimum, undertake appropriate generic ECDIS training, meeting the competence requirements of the 2010 Manila Amendments to the STCW Convention and Code;

(3) the 2010 Manila Amendments to the STCW Convention and Code have reinforced ECDIS training requirements and introduced several additional specific competencies in the use of ECDIS for officers both at management and operational level serving on ECDIS-fitted ships (refer to STCW Code, Tables A-Ⅱ/1 and A-Ⅱ/2). Training in accordance with the 2010 Manila Amendments became effective from 1 July 2013;

(4) masters and officers certificated under chapter Ⅱ of the STCW Convention serving on board ships fitted with ECDIS are to be familiarized (in accordance with STCW Convention, regulation Ⅰ/14) with the ship's equipment including ECDIS;

(5) STCW Convention, regulation Ⅰ/14, paragraph 1.5, as well as section 6.3 of the International Safety Management (ISM) Code, requires companies to ensure seafarers are provided with familiarization. A ship safety management system should include familiarization with the ECDIS equipment fitted, including its backup arrangements, sensors and related peripherals. ECDIS manufacturers are encouraged to provide training resources including type-specific materials. These resources may form part of the ECDIS familiarization;

(6) STCW Convention, regulation Ⅰ/14, paragraph 1.4, requires companies to maintain evidence of the training and ensures that it is readily accessible. For certificates of competency that have expiry dates beyond 1 January 2017, port State control authorities should accept the certificate issued as prima facie

---

① Training and assessment in the use of ECDIS is not required for those who serve exclusively on ships not fitted with ECDIS. This limitation shall be reflected in the endorsements issued to the seafarer concerned (refer to tables A-Ⅱ/1 and A-Ⅱ/2 of the STCW Code).

evidence that the seafarer has met the standard of competence required by the 2010 Amendments in accordance with the control provisions of article X and regulation I/4 of the STCW Convention;

(7) companies should also maintain evidence of the familiarization in compliance with STCW Convention, regulation I/14, paragraph 1.5;

(8) Administrations should inform their port State control officers of the requirements for ECDIS training as detailed in sub-paragraph 6 above; and

(9) attention is also drawn to:

STCW.7/Circ.16—Clarification of transitional provisions relating to the 2010 Manila Amendments to the STCW Convention and Code;

STCW.7/Circ.17—Advice for port State control officers on transitional arrangements leading up to the full implementation of the requirements of the 2010 Manila Amendments to the STCW Convention and Code on 1 January 2017; and

STCW.7/Circ.24/Rev.1—Guidance for Parties, Administrations, port State control authorities, recognized organizations and other relevant parties on the requirements of the STCW Convention, 1978, as amended.

G TRANSITIONING FROM PAPER CHART TO ECDIS NAVIGATION

35 As an initial step, shipowners and operators should undertake an assessment of the issues involved in changing from paper chart to ECDIS navigation. Ships' masters and deck officers should participate in any such assessment so as to capture any practical concerns or needs of those that would be required to use ECDIS. Such a process will help facilitate an early understanding of any issues to be addressed and will help masters and deck officers prepare for change.

36 Documenting the assessment of issues, combined with the development of ECDIS standard operating procedures, will help lead to the adoption of robust ECDIS navigation practices, simplification of masters and deck officers' training and facilitate smooth handovers.

37 In addition, shipowners and operators should ensure that their ships' masters and deck officers are provided with a generic ECDIS training and an ECDIS familiarization programme so that the ships' masters and deck officers fully understand the use of ECDIS for passage planning and navigation.

38 In addition to national and international rules and regulations, IMO model

course 1.27 on Operational Use of Electronic Chart Display and Information Systems (ECDIS) and IMO performance standards, IHO has published an online publication "Facts about electronic charts and carriage requirements". It is a recommended source of information on ECDIS hardware, training and the technical aspects of electronic chart data. Copies are available free of charge from various sources including: https://iho.int/en/standards-and-specifications.

39 Shipowners and operators should always refer to their national Administrations for the latest information on ECDIS carriage and use.

F GUIDANCE ON TRAINING AND ASSESSMENT IN THE OPERATIONAL USE OF ECDIS SIMULATORS

40 When simulators are being used for training or assessment in the operational use of ECDIS, the following interim guidance should be taken into consideration in any such training or assessment.

41 Training and assessment in the operational use of the ECDIS should:

(1) incorporate the use of ECDIS simulation equipment; and

(2) conform to standards not inferior to those given in paragraphs 42 and 43 below.

42 ECDIS simulation equipment should, in addition to meeting all applicable performance standards set out in section A-I/12 of the STCW Code, as amended, be capable of simulating navigational equipment and bridge operational controls which meet all applicable performance standards adopted by the Organization, incorporate facilities to generate soundings and:

(1) create a real-time operating environment, including navigation control and communications instruments and equipment appropriate to the navigation and watchkeeping tasks to be carried out and the manoeuvring skills to be assessed; and

(2) realistically simulate "own ship" characteristics in open-water conditions, as well as the effects of weather, tidal stream and currents.

43 Demonstrations of, and practice in, ECDIS use should be undertaken, where appropriate, through the use of simulators. Training exercises should preferably be undertaken in real time, in order to increase trainees' awareness of the hazards of the improper use of ECDIS. Accelerated timescale may be used only for demonstrations.

44 Detailed guidance is provided in Appendix 3.

APPENDIX 1

LIST OF ECDIS APPARENT OPERATING AND DISPLAY ANOMALIES

(NOT IN PRIORITY ORDER)

In the following list, items 1, 2, 3, 4, 5 (b), 6, 7 and 11 are checked against the IHO DPPC data set dated November 2011:

1   Inability to correctly display symbols for IMO-approved features such as ASLs or PSSAs—ECDIS equipment that does not have the latest version of the IHO Presentation Library installed will, instead of displaying the correct symbol, either show question marks (?) or nothing at all. In some cases the ECDIS may fail to load an ENC that includes such data. An ECDIS retains its type approval certificate regardless of the version of the Presentation Library installed.

   Workaround—interrogate any "?" symbol displayed using the "pick report" or refer to paper charts and/or publications.

2   Incorrect display of foul areas and obstructions in some ECDIS equipment—some ECDIS models do not show some underwater features in standard display mode as expected (however they do activate appropriate alarms). These features are only displayed when the "All" or "Other" display mode is used. Also in some cases different symbols are used to depict these features.

   Workaround—use Mode "All" or "Other".

3   On some occasions some stranded/dangerous wrecks and obstructions may not display in any mode; it is believed that this is limited to some ECDIS versions from a single manufacturer who has now produced a software amendment to resolve the problem.

   Workaround—use paper charts.

4 An object that falls on a contour line may fail to display in "Standard" mode in some ECDIS equipment.

Workaround—use Mode "All" or "Other".

5 Small (point) land areas, especially those depicted only on small-scale (usage band 1 and 2) ENCs may not always be clearly displayed and do not always activate alarms in route planning or route monitoring modes in some ECDIS equipment:

(a) it is possible for small land features to be obscured by other chart detail such as names or contour labels; and

(b) some ECDIS equipment may not conduct route checks on small-scale ENCs and may therefore not provide an appropriate warning. Where this is the case the land area may not be detected by the "look ahead" function during route monitoring.

Workaround—careful manual inspection of the largest scale ENC available.

Due to the limitations of ECDIS referred to in 5 (a) above, mariners (even those using the most modern systems) should always undertake careful visual inspection of the entire planned route using the "Other/All" display mode to confirm that it, and any deviations from it, are clear of dangers.

6 Incorrect display of the coloured arcs of light sectors—some ECDIS may not display the coloured arcs of complex lights as intended. This is especially prevalent where the sectors straddle 0/360 deg (North).

Workaround—use "pick report" function to check light sectors.

7 Some early models of ECDIS are unable to display correctly time-variable data encoded in ENCs. For example features with Date Start and Date End attributes used for the implementation of new traffic routeing measures in ENCs may not be depicted correctly; the result being that both old and new instances are displayed simultaneously. Tests for this were not included in IEC61174 Edition1.

Workaround—use "pick report" function to determine Start/End date/time.

APPENDIX 1   LIST OF ECDIS APPARENT OPERATING AND DISPLAY ANOMALIES (NOT IN PRIORITY ORDER)

8   Tidal stream data not available in usable form—some early models of ECDIS only provide a comma-separated list of values which is difficult to interpret and use.

Workaround—use Tidal Stream Atlases external to ECDIS.

9   Display of anchorage, berth and channel names may not be easily visible to the mariner and the radius of a maximum swinging circle may not be shown.

Workaround—use "All" or "Other" display mode and "pick report" function to obtain swinging circle information; VTS/Port Authority communications will be able to clarify any necessary names.

10   Three hundred and sixty degree landfall lights not always prominent in comparison to shorter range sector lights.

Workaround—mariners to be aware-use "pick report" to verify light characteristic.

11   ENCs may include certain shoal soundings, especially reported depths, which have been encoded in such a way that they do not display in "Standard" mode and might not activate an alarm even where the depth is less than the safety contour setting. Most hydrographic offices have reported to IHO that they have updated the relevant ENCs to ensure that significant depths are displayed in Standard mode.

Workaround—operate in a display mode where all soundings are shown.

12   Areas of foul ground that have no known depth value may be depicted in some ECDIS as isolated dangers and shown in "Standard" mode; this can result in unnecessary screen clutter.

Workaround—no workaround for clutter problem, mariners to be aware and use "pick report" function to determine if the feature is a danger.

13   Where ECDIS includes an option to show isolated dangers in waters shoaler than the safety contour value the symbology used may vary between manufacturers.

Workaround—mariners to be aware and to use "All" or "Other" Mode when operating in such areas.

14 Screen clutter can be a problem when displaying smaller scale ENCs for areas where larger scale coverage is also loaded in ECDIS. This can be more apparent when the user zooms out. This is due to a combination of each manufacturer's ENC loading strategy and the individual ENC producer's encoding policy. Where hydrographic offices use SCAMIN (scale minimum) attributes on chart features then this problem is minimized. The intention of the IHO standard is that ECDIS should not display ENC data which has a compilation scale significantly different from the display scale in use. Improvements could be made, in future, by adopting a standardized ENC loading strategy based on a scale range defined within the ENC.

Workaround—the situation can be improved through use of the standard display mode during voyage monitoring and appropriate (but not over) use of the zoom function. This technique has been included in the syllabus of IMO model course 1.27 on Operational Use of Electronic Chart Display and Information Systems (ECDIS).

15 In some ECDIS equipment the text for some notes in the ENC may be truncated or not displayed at all, and therefore is not available to the mariner.

Workaround—no workaround available; mariners should advise ENC service providers where they observe this problem.

16 Unnecessary alarms and indications—feedback from mariners shows that ECDIS can produce excessive and distracting alarms. This is due to a combination of the interpretation of the requirements of the ECDIS Performance Standards and the ENC encoding. Some control over the number of alarms and indications is available to the mariner in ECDIS built to the revised Performance Standards [resolution MSC.232 (82)], but this is not always recognized.

Workaround—the methods available to minimize alarms are included in the syllabus of IMO model course 1.27 on Operational Use of Electronic Chart Display and Information Systems (ECDIS).

APPENDIX 2

DIFFERENCES BETWEEN RASTER CHART DISPLAY SYSTEM (RCDS) AND ECDIS

The mariners' attention is drawn to the following limitations of the RCDS mode:

1 Unlike ENC, where there are no displayed boundaries, RNCs are based on paper charts and as such have boundaries which are evident in ECDIS;

2 RNCs will not trigger automatic alarms (e.g. anti-grounding). However, alarms and indications can be generated with the manual addition, during passage planning, e.g. of clearing lines, ship safety contour lines, isolated danger markers and danger areas to mitigate these limitations;

3 Horizontal datums and chart projections may differ between RNCs. Mariners should understand how a chart's horizontal datum relates to the datum of the position fixing system in use. In some instances, this may appear as a shift in position. This difference may be most noticeable at grid intersections;

4 A number of RNCs cannot be referenced to either WGS-84 or PE 90 geodetic datums. Where this is the case, ECDIS should give a continuous indication;

5 The display of RNCs features cannot be simplified by the removal of features to suit a particular navigational circumstance or task at hand. This could affect the superimposition of radar/ARPA;

6 Without selecting different scale charts the look ahead capability may be limited. This may lead to inconvenience when determining range and bearing or the identity of distant objects;

7 Orientation of the RCDS display to other than chart-up, may affect the readability of chart text and symbols (e.g. course-up, route-up);

8 It is not possible to interrogate RNC features to gain additional information about charted objects. Whether using ENC or RNC, in the planning process a mariner should consult all relevant publications (such as sailing directions, etc.);

9 With RNC, it is not possible to display a ship's safety contour or safety depth and highlight it on the display unless these features are manually entered during route planning;

10 Depending on the source of the RNC, different colours may be used to

show similar chart information. There may also be differences in colours used during day and night-time;

11　A RNC is intended to be used at the scale of the equivalent paper chart. Excessive zooming in or zooming out can seriously degrade the displayed image. If the RNC is displayed at a larger scale than the equivalent paper chart, the ECDIS will provide an indication; and

12　ECDIS provides an indication in the ENC which allows a determination of the quality of hydrographic the data. When using RNCs, mariners are invited to consult the source diagram or the zone of confidence diagram, if available.

APPENDIX 3

GUIDANCE ON TRAINING AND ASSESSMENT IN THE OPERATIONAL USE OF ECDIS SIMULATORS

GENERAL

Goals of an ECDIS training programme

1 The ECDIS trainee should be able to:

(1) operate the ECDIS equipment, use the navigational functions of ECDIS, select and assess all relevant information and take proper action in the case of a malfunction;

(2) state the potential errors of displayed data and the usual errors of interpretation; and

(3) explain why ECDIS should not be relied upon as the sole reliable aid to navigation.

Theory and demonstration

2 As the safe use of ECDIS requires knowledge and understanding of the basic principles governing ECDIS data and their presentation rules as well as potential errors in displayed data and ECDIS-related limitations and potential dangers, a number of lectures covering the theoretical explanation should be provided. As far as possible, such lessons should be presented within a familiar context and make use of practical examples. They should be reinforced during simulator exercises.

3 For safe operation of ECDIS equipment and ECDIS-related information (use of the navigational functions of ECDIS, selection and assessment of all relevant information, becoming familiar with ECDIS man-machine interfacing), practical exercises and training on the ECDIS simulators should constitute the main content of

the course.

4　For the definition of training objectives, a structure of activities should be defined. A detailed specification of learning objectives should be developed for each topic of this structure.

Simulator exercises

5　Exercises should be carried out on individual ECDIS simulators, or full-mission navigation simulators including ECDIS, to enable trainees to acquire the necessary practical skills. For real-time navigation exercises, navigation simulators are recommended to cover the complex navigation situation. The exercises should provide training in the use of the various scales, navigational modes, and display modes which are available, so that the trainees will be able to adapt the use of the equipment to the particular situation concerned.

6　The choice of exercises and scenarios is governed by the simulator facilities available. If one or more ECDIS workstations and a full-mission simulator are available, the workstations may primarily be used for basic exercises in the use of ECDIS facilities and for passage-planning exercises, whereas full-mission simulators may primarily be used for exercises related to passage-monitoring functions in real time, as realistic as possible in connection with the total workload of a navigational watch. The degree of complexity of exercises should increase throughout the training programme until the trainee has mastered all aspects of the learning subject.

7　Exercises should produce the greatest impression of realism. To achieve this, the scenarios could be located in a fictitious sea area. Situations, functions and actions for different learning objectives which occur in different sea areas can be integrated into one exercise and experienced in real time.

8　The main objective of simulator exercises is to ensure that trainees understand their responsibilities in the operational use of ECDIS in all safety-relevant aspects and are thoroughly familiar with the system and equipment used.

Principal types of ECDIS and their display characteristics

9　The trainee should gain knowledge of the principal types of ECDIS in use; their various display characteristics, data structure and an understanding of:

（1）differences between vector and raster charts;

APPENDIX 3　GUIDANCE ON TRAINING AND ASSESSMENT
IN THE OPERATIONAL USE OF ECDIS SIMULATORS

(2) differences between ECDIS and ECS;

(3) differences between ECDIS and RCDS;

(4) characteristics of different types of ECDIS; and

(5) characteristics of systems for special purposes (unusual situations/emergencies).

Risks of over-reliance on ECDIS

10　The training in ECDIS operational use should address:

(1) the limitations of ECDIS as a navigational tool;

(2) potential risk of improper functioning of the system;

(3) system limitations, including those of its sensors;

(4) hydrographic data inaccuracy; limitations of vector and raster electronic charts (ECDIS *vs.* RCDS and ENC *vs.* RNC); and

(5) potential risk of human errors.

Emphasis should be placed on the need to keep a proper lookout and to perform periodical checking, especially of the ship's position, by ECDIS-independent methods.

Detection of misrepresentation of information

11　Knowledge of the limitations of the equipment and detection of misrepresentation of information is essential for the safe use of ECDIS. The following factors should be emphasized during training:

(1) performance standards of the equipment;

(2) radar data representation on an electronic chart, elimination of discrepancy between the radar image and the electronic chart;

(3) possible projection discrepancies between an electronic and paper charts;

(4) possible scale discrepancies (overscaling and underscaling) in displaying an electronic chart and its original scale;

(5) effects of using different reference systems for positioning;

(6) effects of using different horizontal and vertical datums;

(7) effects of the motion of the ship in a seaway;

(8) ECDIS limitations in raster chart display mode;

(9) potential errors in the display of:

①the own ship's position;

②radar data and ARPA and AIS information;

③different geodetic coordinate systems; and

(10) verification of the results of manual or automatic data correction:

①comparison of chart data and radar picture; and

②checking the own ship's position by using other independent position-fixing systems.

12 False interpretation of the data and proper action to be taken to avoid errors of interpretation, should be explained. The implications of the following should be emphasized:

(1) ignoring overscaling of the display;

(2) uncritical acceptance of the own ship's position;

(3) confusion of display mode;

(4) confusion of chart scale;

(5) confusion of reference systems;

(6) different modes of presentation;

(7) different modes of vector stabilization;

(8) differences between true north and gyro north (radar);

(9) using the same data reference system;

(10) using the appropriate chart scale;

(11) using the best-suited sensor to the given situation and circumstances;

(12) entering the correct values of safety data:

①the own ship's safety contour;

②safety depth (safe water); and

③events; and

(13) proper use of all available data.

13 Appreciation that RCDS is only a navigational aid and that, when operating in the RCDS mode, the ECDIS equipment should be used together with an appropriate portfolio of up-to-date paper charts:

(1) appreciation of the differences in operation of RCDS mode as described in appendix 2; and

(2) ECDIS, in any mode, should be used in training with an appropriate portfolio of up-to-date charts.

APPENDIX 3 GUIDANCE ON TRAINING AND ASSESSMENT
IN THE OPERATIONAL USE OF ECDIS SIMULATORS

Factors affecting system performance and accuracy

14 An elementary understanding should be attained of the principles of ECDIS, together with a full practical knowledge of:

(1) starting and setting up ECDIS; connecting data sensors: satellite and radio navigation system receivers, radar, gyro-compass, log, echo-sounder; accuracy and limitations of these sensors, including effects of measurement errors and ship's position accuracy, manoeuvring on the accuracy of course indicator's performance, compass error on the accuracy of course indication, shallow water on the accuracy of log performance, log correction on the accuracy of speed calculation, disturbance (sea state) on the accuracy of an echo-sounder performance; and

(2) the current performance standards for electronic chart display and information systems adopted by the Organization. ①

Practice

Setting up and maintaining display

15 Knowledge and skills should be attained in:

(1) the correct starting procedure to obtain the optimum display of ECDIS information;

(2) the selection of display presentation (standard display, display base, all other information displayed individually on demand);

(3) the correct adjustment of all variable radar/ARPA display controls for optimum display of data;

(4) the selection of convenient configuration;

(5) the selection, as appropriate, of required speed input to ECDIS;

(6) the selection of the timescale of vectors; and

(7) performance checks of position, radar/ARPA, compass, speed input sensors and ECDIS.

---

① See relevant/appropriate performance standards adopted by the Organization.

Operational use of electronic charts

16　Knowledge and skills should be attained in:

(1) the main characteristics of the display of ECDIS data and selecting proper information for navigational tasks;

(2) the automatic functions required for monitoring ship's safety, such as display of position, heading/gyro course, speed, safety values and time;

(3) the manual functions (by the cursor, electronic bearing line, range rings);

(4) selecting and modification of electronic chart content;

(5) scaling (including underscaling and overscaling);

(6) zooming;

(7) setting of the own ship's safety data;

(8) using a daytime or nighttime display mode;

(9) reading all chart symbols and abbreviations;

(10) using different kinds of cursors and electronic bars for obtaining navigational data;

(11) viewing an area in different directions and returning to the ship's position;

(12) finding the necessary area, using geographical coordinates;

(13) displaying indispensable data layers appropriate to a navigational situation;

(14) selecting appropriate and unambiguous data (position, course, speed, etc.);

(15) entering the mariner's notes;

(16) using north-up orientation presentation and other kinds of orientation; and

(17) using true- and relative-motion modes.

Route planning

17　Knowledge and skills should be attained in:

(1) loading the ship's characteristics into ECDIS;

(2) selection of a sea area for route planning:

　　①reviewing required waters for the sea passage; and

　　②changing over of chart scale;

APPENDIX 3 GUIDANCE ON TRAINING AND ASSESSMENT IN THE OPERATIONAL USE OF ECDIS SIMULATORS

③ verifying that proper and updated charts are available;

④ route planning on a display by means of ECDIS, using the graphic editor, taking into consideration rhumb line and great-circle sailing:

.1 using the ECDIS database for obtaining navigational, hydrometeorological and other data;

.2 taking into consideration turning radius and wheel-over points/lines when they are displayed on chart scale;

.3 marking dangerous depths and areas and exhibiting guarding depth contours;

.4 marking waypoints with the crossing depth contours and critical cross track deviations, as well as by adding, replacing and erasing of waypoints;

.5 taking into consideration safe speed;

.6 checking pre-planned route for navigational safety; and

.7 generating alarms and warnings;

⑤ route planning with calculation in the table format, including:

.1 waypoints selection;

.2 recalling the waypoints list;

.3 planning notes;

.4 adjustment of a planned route;

.5 checking a pre-planned route for navigational safety;

.6 alternative route planning;

.7 saving planned routes, loading and unloading or deleting routes;

.8 making a graphic copy of the monitor screen and printing a route;

.9 editing and modification of the planned route;

.10 setting of safety values according to the size and manoeuvring parameters of the vessel;

.11 back-route planning; and

.12 connecting several routes.

Route monitoring

18 Knowledge and skills should be attained in:

(1) using independent data to control ship's position or using alternative systems within ECDIS;

(2) using the look ahead function:

①changing charts and their scales;

②reviewing navigational charts;

③vector time selecting;

④predicting the ship's position for some time interval;

⑤changing the pre-planned route (route modification);

⑥entering independent data for the calculation of wind drift and current allowance;

⑦reacting properly to the alarm;

⑧entering corrections for discrepancies of the geodetic datum;

⑨displaying time markers on a ship's route;

⑩entering ship's position manually; and

⑪measuring coordinates, course, bearings and distances on a chart.

Alarm handling

19 Knowledge and ability to interpret and react properly to all kinds of alarm systems, such as navigational sensors, indicators, data and charts alarms and indicator warnings, including, switching the sound and visual alarm signalling system on/off, should be attained in case of:

(1) absence of the next chart in the ECDIS database;

(2) crossing a safety contour;

(3) exceeding cross track limits;

(4) deviation from planned route;

(5) approaching a waypoint;

(6) approaching a critical point;

(7) discrepancy between calculated and actual time of arrival to a waypoint;

(8) information on underscaling or overscaling;

(9) approaching an isolated navigational danger or danger area;

(10) crossing a specified area;

(11) selecting a different geodetic datum;

(12) approaching other ships;

(13) watch termination;

(14) switching timer;

(15) system test failure;

APPENDIX 3   GUIDANCE ON TRAINING AND ASSESSMENT
IN THE OPERATIONAL USE OF ECDIS SIMULATORS

(16) malfunctioning of the positioning system used in ECDIS;

(17) failure of dead reckoning; and

(18) inability to fix vessel's position using the navigational system.

Manual correction of a ship's position and motion parameters

20   Knowledge and skills should be attained in manually correcting:

(1) the ship's position in dead reckoning mode, when the satellite and radio navigation system receiver is switched off;

(2) the ship's position, when automatically obtained coordinates are inaccurate; and

(3) course and speed values.

Records in the ship's log

21   Knowledge and skills should be attained in:

(1) automatic voyage recording;

(2) reconstruction of past track, taking into account:

①recording media;

②recording intervals;

③verification of database in use;

(3) viewing records in the electronic ship's log;

(4) instant recording in the electronic ship's log;

(5) changing ship's time;

(6) entering the additional data;

(7) printing the content of the electronic ship's log;

(8) setting up the automatic record time intervals;

(9) composition of voyage data and reporting; and

(10) interface with a voyage data recorder (VDR).

Chart updating

22   Knowledge and skills should be attained in:

(1) performing manual updating of electronic charts. Special attention should be paid to reference ellipsoid conformity and to conformity of the measurement units

used on a chart and in the correction text;

(2) performing semi-automatic updating of electronic charts, using the data obtained on electronic media in the electronic chart format; and

(3) performing automatic updating of electronic charts, using update files obtained via electronic data communication lines.

In the scenarios where non-updated data are employed to create a critical situation, trainees should be required to perform ad hoc updating of the chart.

Operational use of ECDIS where radar/ARPA is connected

23　Knowledge and skills should be attained in:

(1) connecting ARPA to ECDIS;

(2) indicating target's speed vectors;

(3) indicating target's tracks;

(4) archiving target's tracks;

(5) viewing the table of the targets;

(6) checking alignment of radar overlay with charted geographic features;

(7) simulating one or more manoeuvres;

(8) corrections to own ship's position, using a reference point captured by ARPA; and

(9) corrections using the ARPA's cursor and electronic bar.

See also STCW Code section B-I/12, Guidance regarding the use of simulators (pertaining to radar and ARPA), especially paragraphs 17 to 19 and 36 to 38.

Operational use of ECDIS where AIS is connected

24　Knowledge and skills should be attained in:

(1) interface with AIS;

(2) interpretation of AIS data;

(3) indicating target's speed vectors;

(4) indicating target's tracks; and

(5) archiving target's tracks.

Operational warnings, their benefits and limitations

25 Trainees should gain an appreciation of the uses, benefits and limitations of ECDIS operational warnings and their correct setting, where applicable, to avoid spurious interference.

System operational tests

26 Knowledge and skills should be attained in:
(1) methods of testing for malfunctions of ECDIS, including functional self-testing;
(2) precautions to be taken after a malfunction occurs; and
(3) adequate backup arrangements (take over and navigate using the backup system).

Debriefing exercise

27 The instructor should analyse the results of all exercises completed by all trainees and print them out. The time spent on the debriefing should take between 10% and 15% of the total time used for simulator exercises.

APPENDIX 4

EXAMPLES OF ONBOARD ECDIS UPDATES

In the following, examples of onboard ECDIS updates and documentation are provided:

Example 1
The TAC lists the release number for software 5.03.xx and the current manufacturer software release number is 5.03.02 and is to be updated to 5.03.03.

Manufacturer Report: The manufacturer reports small bug fixes or changes for the last digit of the IHO standards.

TAA decision: The TAA decides that the reported changes are minor changes and do not need re-certification or LOA.

Documents provided: The old TAC, DOC.

The software release number changes from 5.03.02 to 5.03.03 which is covered by 5.03.xx in the existing TAC.

Example 2
The TAC lists the release number for software 5.03.xx and the current manufacturer software release number is 5.03.02 and is to be updated to 5.04.00.

Manufacturer Report: The manufacturer reports additional functionality or changes in existing functionality.

TAA decision: The TAA decides that the changes are TAC relevant and requires additional testing and consequential re-certification.

Documents provided: New TAC, new DOC.

The software release number changes from 5.03.02 to 5.04.00 and 5.04.xx is taken over into the new TAC.

Example 3
The TAC lists the IHO standard edition 3.0.x and the current manufacturer IHO standard edition is 3.0.(1) and is required to be updated to edition 3.1.(0).

APPENDIX 4 EXAMPLES OF ONBOARD ECDIS UPDATES

Manufacturer Report: The manufacturer reports updates to meet the latest IHO requirements.

TAA decision: The TAA decides that the changes are a major change and TAC relevant and requires retesting.

Documents provided: The old TAC supplemented by an LOA, new DOC.

The IHO standard edition changing from 3.0.(1) to 3.1.(0) is mentioned in the LOA.

Example 4

Manufacturer manufactures ECDIS with software version 5.0, and then changes the manufacturing to software version 6.0. The hardware remains unchanged. In this case a new TAC listing v6.0.xx replaces the previous TAC listing v5.0.xx.

Manufacturer Report: The manufacturer reports software updates from 5.0 to 6.0.

TAA decision: The TAA decides that the changes are a major change and TAC relevant and requires re-certification.

Documents provided: New TAC, new DOC.

The software release number changes from 5.0 to 6.0 in the new TAC.

REFERENCES

IMO PERFORMANCE STANDARDS FOR ECDIS

1　RESOLUTION A. 817 (19): PERFORMANCE STANDARDS FOR ELECTRONIC CHART DISPLAY AND INFORMATION SYSTEMS (ECDIS)

2　RESOLUTION MSC. 64 (67): RECOMMENDATIONS ON NEW AND AMENDED PERFORMANCE STANDARDS

3　RESOLUTION MSC. 86 (70): ADOPTION OF NEW AND AMENDED PERFORMANCE STANDARDS FOR NAVIGATIONAL EQUIPMENT

4　RESOLUTION MSC. 232 (82): ADOPTION OF THE REVISED PERFORMANCE STANDARDS FOR ELECTRONIC CHART DISPLAY AND INFORMATION SYSTEMS (ECDIS)

5　RESOLUTION MSC. 530 (106) /Rev. 1: PERFORMANCE STANDARDS FOR ELECTRONIC CHART DISPLAY AND INFORMATION SYSTEMS (ECDIS)

OTHER IMO CIRCULARS RELATED TO ECDIS

1　MSC. 1/Circ. 982: GUIDELINES ON ERGONOMIC CRITERIA FOR BRIDGE EQUIPMENT AND LAYOUT

2　MSC. 1/Circ. 1091: ISSUES TO BE CONSIDERED WHEN INTRODUCING NEW TECHNOLOGY ON BOARD SHIP

3　MSC. 1/Circ. 1221: VALIDITY OF TYPE APPROVAL CERTIFICATION FOR MARINE PRODUCTS

4　MSC. 1/Circ. 1389: GUIDANCE ON PROCEDURES FOR UPDATING SHIPBORNE NAVIGATION AND COMMUNICATION EQUIPMENT

5　SN. 1/Circ. 213: GUIDANCE ON CHART DATUMS AND THE ACCURACY OF POSITIONS ON CHARTS

6　SN. 1/Circ. 243/Rev. 1 AMENDED GUIDELINES FOR THE PRESENTATION OF NAVIGATIONAL-RELATED SYMBOLS, TERMS AND ABBREVIATIONS

7　SN. 1/Circ. 255: ADDITIONAL GUIDANCE ON CHART DATUMS AND

REFERENCES

THE ACCURACY OF POSITIONS ON CHARTS

8 SN. 1/Circ. 265: GUIDELINES ON THE APPLICATION OF SOLAS REGULATION V/15 TO INS, IBS AND BRIDGE DESIGN

9 SN. 1/Circ. 288: GUIDELINES FOR BRIDGE EQUIPMENT AND SYSTEMS, THEIR ARRANGEMENT AND INTEGRATION (BES)